THE
NINE BAD SHOTS
OF GOLF
and what to do about them

JIM DANTE, *Five Times President*
New Jersey P.G.A.

and

LEO DIEGEL, *Twice American P.G.A.*
Champion and Four Times Canadian
Open Champion

in collaboration with

LEN ELLIOTT, *Sports Editor*
Newark Evening News

A FIRESIDE BOOK
PUBLISHED BY SIMON & SCHUSTER INC.
New York   London   Toronto   Sydney   Tokyo   Singapore

FIRESIDE
Simon & Schuster Building
Rockefeller Center
1230 Avenue of the Americas
New York, New York 10020

Published by arrangement with McGraw-Hill Publishing
Company

FIRESIDE and colophon are registered trademarks
of Simon & Schuster Inc.

Manufactured in the United States of America

10 9 8 7 6 5 4 3 2 1   Pbk.

Library of Congress Cataloging in Publication Data

Dante, Jim.
     The nine bad shots of golf and what to do about
them/Jim Dante and Leo Diegel, in collaboration with
Len Elliott.
     p. cm.
     "A Fireside book."
     1. Golf. I. Diegel, Leo. II. Elliott, Len. III. Title.
IV. Title: 9 bad shots of golf and what to do about them.
GV965.D339   1990   90-30735
796.352'3—dc20   CIP

ISBN 0-671-70718-3 Pbk.

INTRODUCTION

This is not a book on "how to play golf."

This is, instead, a book designed to help you help yourself. In short, it is to "straighten you out."

If we could, we'd all like to take a professional with us on every round, and when we began to hit some bad shots he would tell us what was wrong and how to correct it. But how many of us are able to do that?

This book, carefully indexed for each bad shot you possibly can hit, attempts to take the place of the pro so far as that is possible. There is, of course, no perfect substitute for him and for the personal instruction he alone is able to give.

There is, however, a reason for every bad shot a golfer hits. It is caused by some fault in his swing. Those faults will produce the same bad shot *every time*. And, conversely, the bad shot—whichever one it happens to be—will be caused by the *same faults* every time.

Therefore, when you find yourself hitting any particular type of bad shot frequently, you can turn to the chapter on that shot in the book and discover why you hit it and how to eliminate the faults that produced it. Once rid of those faults, you will not hit that kind of shot again.

How is it possible thus to simplify things? Because, contrary to what you may have thought, there are not a thousand bad shots in golf.

There are only nine.

Incredible, isn't it?

But, besides hitting a straight ball, what can you do? You can hook, you can slice, you can push, pull, sky, top, sclaff, smother, or shank a shot. Nothing else. Just nine.

INTRODUCTION

Suppose, for instance, that you are hooking. Opening the book to the chapter on hooking, you find out, first, what causes a hook. To be more specific, you find that hooking is caused by hitting with a closed face. You then go on to find the faults that cause a closed face. You check yourself on those faults carefully. You eliminate them from your swing and—lo, the hook disappears.

Of course, a golfer who is badly deficient in the fundamentals, who uses the wrong grip, the wrong stance, and has a swing that never was meant for the game, can't just consult one of the corrective chapters and clear up all his troubles. It's not that easy. He will have to spend some time on Part I, The Fundamentals. For many golfers, Part I alone will solve a multitude of difficulties.

There are thousands of golfers, however, who play in the low 90's and high 80's, who have pretty good swings, and who do almost everything right. They are held back by some fault that, although slight, is persistent and that they can't detect.

These players usually hit one type of bad shot consistently. One of them, for instance, may be a chronic hooker, another an habitual slicer, but seldom are they all over the course, uncontrollably wild. These players should be able to discover the flaws in their swings by a study of the fundamentals and then straighten out their bad shots through the particular chapters devoted to them.

Certain mistakes also crop up habitually in the shorter shots, such as short pitches, chips, putts, and shots from sand traps and the rough. These mistakes and the faults that cause them likewise have been dealt with, so that we believe the game has been covered from tee to green from the standpoint of its bad shots.

We hope it has, and we hope the remedies we have given you for your bad shots will help you. If you follow the instructions closely and carefully, we know they will.

JIM DANTE
LEO DIEGEL

CONTENTS

Introduction

PART 1

1. Grip and Stance 3
2. The Swing 16

PART 2

3. Slicing 43
4. Hooking 60
5. Topping 71
6. Smothering 84
7. Pulling 91
8. Pushing 98
9. Skying 105
10. Sclaffing 113
11. Shanking 120

PART 3

12. Iron Play 129
13. Putting 141
14. Out of the Rough and Traps 157
15. Uneven Lies 165

PART 4

16. General Observations and Conclusions . . . 173
Index 186

PART ONE

CHAPTER ONE

GRIP AND STANCE

THE MANNER in which you place your hands on the club and your position as you address the ball are both highly important. Yet the average golfer pays little attention to either one.

The grip is important because it is the connecting link between the club and the person who swings the club. If the grip is correct you will have little difficulty in bringing the face of the club head against the ball while the face is at right angles to the line of flight, neither open nor closed. That's the way it must be for a good shot.

Furthermore, the correct grip provides insurance against the stronger right hand (in a right-handed person) overpowering the left as the club meets the ball, thereby spoiling the shot.

GRIP

The grip itself is so important that we shall make the following statement without fear of contradiction: The best professional today, using any one of many grips that we see in Sunday morning foursomes, won't break 80. And when a pro doesn't break 80 he's about ready to hang himself.

How, then, can you expect to break 100 or even 90 using the same grip?

So let's get to the right grip.

3

In the first place, the club is held in the palm and fingers of the left hand and in the fingers of the right. That's a basic fundamental. Don't forget it or try to hold the club any other way. Hold it in the palm and fingers of the left hand and in the fingers of the right.

Now it's easy to think you are holding the club in the palm and fingers of the left when actually it's in the fingers alone. So make this test. Grip the club and address the ball. Then stop. Take your right hand off the club and, still keeping the grip with the left, turn the left hand until the palm is up. Raise the club until it is parallel with the ground. Then grasp the shaft with the right hand and press it down on the palm of the left. Now, with the shaft held down hard against the left hand, open the left hand and see where the shaft lies. Is it in the palm? Can you see any of the palm between the shaft and your fingers? If you can, fine. That's where you want it. But if you see no palm, then you have only a finger grip with the left hand and that's bad.

Incidentally, the fact that the pros develop big calluses at the bases of the little finger and third finger of the left hand is because there is a fold of skin from the palm between the shaft and the fingers.

Now, in placing the left hand on the club with the palm and finger grip, place it so that the big knuckles of the first three fingers are visible as you address the ball. If the left hand is so far on top of the shaft that the knuckle of the fourth finger is visible, it is too much on top. If less than three knuckles can be seen, the left hand is too far to the left. The left thumb simply goes down the shaft naturally.

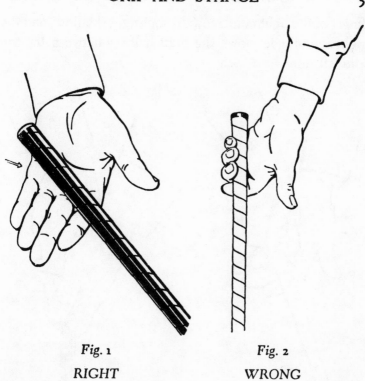

Fig. 1   Fig. 2

RIGHT   WRONG

*Figs. 1 and 2. Here we see the correct and incorrect ways of grip-ping with the left hand. In the correct grip the shaft lies diagonally across the palm and fingers. Arrow shows the part of palm that will fold against shaft when hand closes. Shown at the right is the grip so many use, with the club held entirely in the fingers. This grip **is** weak compared with the palm-and-finger method.*

Now for the right hand.

The right hand merely fits on the shaft against the left, the little finger of the right overlapping the first finger of the left. The V formed by the opening between the thumb and first finger of the right points toward your right shoulder, and the right thumb goes down the shaft halfway between the top and left side.

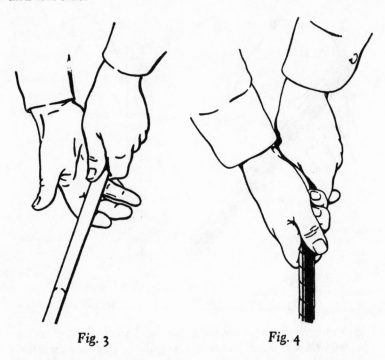

Fig. 3   Fig. 4

Figs. 3 and 4.   In Fig. 3 the left hand has completed its grip, and the right hand is being placed on the shaft. This shows the right hand gripping with the three fingers alone, with the little finger about to overlap the first finger of the left hand. Figure 4 shows the completed grip. Here the V's formed by the thumb and forefinger of each hand are pointing in the same direction—toward the right shoulder. The little finger of the right can be seen overlapping the forefinger of the left. The grip looks strong and firm.

That is the overlapping, or Vardon, grip. And it's the best. Harry Vardon, the great English professional, may not have been the first to use it but he popularized it. And Vardon was truly great. He was good enough to win the British Open six times and was also good enough, at the age of fifty, to tie for second place in the American Open of 1920 with Leo Diegel, Jock Hutchison, and Jack Burke. Bob Jones and countless others have used the same grip.

The overlapping grip with the hands in the position described is the best that has been devised for enabling the player to bring the face of the club to the ball at right angles to the line of flight. It does this because as the hands are placed on the club they are in a natural, unstrained position. There is no twisting of either wrist that will cause an untwisting at some point in the swing. Any such untwisting will tend to either close or open the club face and produce crooked shots.

This grip also brings the club head to the top of the swing *half* closed as it should be when the proper wrist action is applied. No other position of the hands will do that.

Take, for example, the following grip. Use the same overlap but move both hands well around to the right so that the left hand is on top of the shaft and the right hand under it. Now make your backswing and look at the club face at the top. It will be tightly closed. The face will be pointing directly at the sky. When you come down to the ball from that position, the face also will be closed, or even hooded, and you will get a bad hook or a smother. Come down to the ball stopping the club before contact, and see for yourself that the face is closed.

Take the overlap again, but with the hands well around to the left. Go to the top with that grip and look at the club face. It will be wide open. If you swing down to the ball from that position, the face will be open at impact and you will get a bad slice. Try that one too, stopping the club at the ball.

Again, put the left hand well to the left and the right hand to the right and under the shaft. Maybe you think nobody ever does this, that it is a gross exaggeration. We can assure you it isn't. We've seen many a duffer try to get results with it. Go to the top with that grip and see what happens. The face will be more than open, and you won't be able to keep your left arm even reasonably straight.

No, the overlapping grip, with the V's pointing toward or just inside the right shoulder, is the best. With the V's in this position there is the least possible strain on the wrists, the least possible chance of either opening or closing the face of the club.

There is one more important point. With the palm-and-finger grip the left hand will grip the club more tightly than the right hand. The right hand steadies the club and guides it. The right also will deliver the punch at the right moment just before impact, but you don't have to worry about that. The right will do that voluntarily. The only thing that concerns you is that the right doesn't deliver too heavy a punch or deliver it too soon. A palm-and-finger grip with the left, which gives that hand more power, will take care of that.

A final and warning word: Keep this grip throughout the

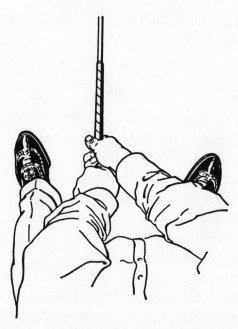

Fig. 5. Here the artist has done an unusual job, showing how the correct grip looks to the player himself. The right hand is in a natural, unstrained position, neither too far to the right nor to the left. Most important, however, is that the knuckles at the bases of the first, second, and third fingers of the left hand can be seen clearly. This means the left is in exactly the right position.

swing. Don't let the left hand open, even a little bit, at the top of the swing. And don't let the club, at the top of the swing, drop into the V between the right thumb and fore-finger. Either one will affect the course of the club head on the downswing. Remember, always, that if the left hand loosens at any point or if the left arm collapses at the elbow, any kind of a bad shot can be produced and almost certainly will be. Keep the grip firm and fixed throughout, as if the hands were molded to the club.

STANCE

Standing up to the ball as you address it should be anything but difficult. Yet, from the positions you see on any given tee, the average golfer makes of it a highly complicated, unnatural, and even grotesque job.

Stand up to the ball naturally. Spread your feet only until they are about as far apart as the width of your shoulders. Stand reasonably erect. Now bend the knees ever so slightly. That's your position from the waist down.

As to the upper part of your body, the idea simply is this. Stand as erect as the length of the club will permit you when you are standing the correct distance from the ball.

That may sound a little complex, but it really isn't.

Set the club head squarely behind the ball with the ball situated opposite your left heel. When the distance between the end of the shaft and your left leg is equal to the distance between the tip of your index finger and the tip of your little finger extended, you are standing the correct distance from the ball. You are standing neither too close nor too far away.

Address the ball, and then make that little test. Take your right hand off the shaft. Spread the fingers as far as you can and, holding them spread, see if you can get them between the end of the shaft and your left leg. If you can't, then you're standing too close. Move away a little. If there is room to spare, you're too far away. Move up.

Fig. 6. Here is a front view of the stance. Notice the firmness of the left arm and hand, the even distribution of weight, and the position of the ball. A slight, conscious firming of the left arm before starting the backswing helps put the left in command from the beginning, as it should be. Dotted line shows that the ball is played, for a full shot, just inside the left heel.

Fig. 7. *Comfort is the keynote here in this side view of the stance. The player is not bending over sharply and is not reaching for the ball. He is in an easy, relaxed position with knees bent slightly and he is perfectly balanced between ball and heel of foot.*

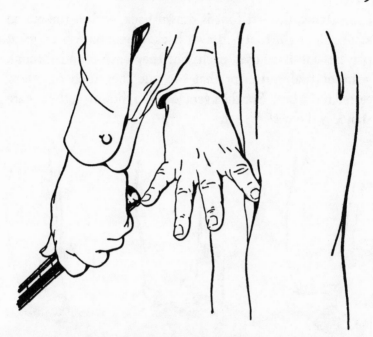

Fig. 8. Here is the test to find out whether you are standing too close or too far away. Player has spread fingers of right hand to measure distance between left leg and end of shaft. If he couldn't get his fingers in this space, he would be standing too close. If he couldn't span the gap he would be standing too far away. Distance here is exactly right.

But once you have found the correct distance by this test, stand as erect as you can. Your body will be inclined forward a little but not much. Help it out by stretching your arms slightly too. You'll be surprised how straight you can stand.

As to using the open stance, the square stance, or the closed stance, we recommend the square, that is, with the feet an equal distance from the projected line of flight. In the open stance the left foot is drawn back, and in the closed stance the right foot is drawn back. There have been great players who have used each, but they have found through years of trial and error that the one they used somehow suited them best. For the average golfer, however, the square stance is the best. Use it.

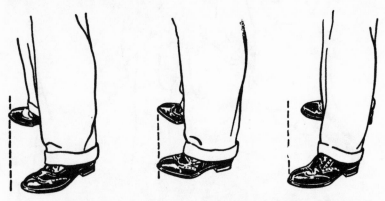

Fig. 9. Three ways to stand up to the ball. Open stance is at left, with left foot drawn back slightly. In closed stance, at right, right foot is back. Square stance is shown in the center.

As to the distribution of weight, you may have been urged at various stages of your troubles to keep your weight on your heels. That is only an antidote, or cure, for the golfer who keeps too much weight on the balls of his feet. He sometimes tends to fall into his shot. But keeping your weight on your heels isn't necessary. Keep it evenly distributed. Have the feeling that you are gripping the ground with your whole foot.

The main object in the stance is to get in as natural, as

easy, as balanced a position as possible. Tension is the worst enemy of the golf swing. If you start the swing tense or rigid, you will make a complete botch of it. If you can stay relaxed and balanced, you are off to a good start. You are not handicapping yourself.

If you are standing too far from the ball, for example, you are forced to bend sharply at the waist. You immediately set up a tension in your muscles that is present in any bending position. Your balance is also destroyed.

Worse still, you immediately put yourself in a position that leads to many of the common faults, such as having too much weight on the left leg at the top of the swing, dipping the left knee, dropping the left shoulder, swaying, lifting and moving the head, bending the left elbow, etc. All these faulty positions can come from bending over to reach the ball, which you will do if you stand too far from it. None will be caused by standing too close to it. Obviously the correct distance is the one to take, but between the two extremes actually it is better to stand too close than too far away.

Similarly, if you spread your feet too far apart in the address, you are assuming an unnatural position—a position that immediately sets up tension. A wide stance also restricts your pivot, which prevents the club head from coming back and around properly on the inside line it should follow. Try it. Take an abnormally wide stance and see if you can turn your hips easily. There is bound to be a marked restriction. Only with a free pivot at the hips and a full shoulder turn can you reach the proper position at the top of the swing.

Taken by and large, the grip and the stance are not difficult. They are only as hard as we make them.

CHAPTER TWO

THE SWING

ONCE THE proper grip and stance are taken, you are ready to swing the club. But you can't just swing it any way you feel like. There are certain fundamentals to be observed or you will hit a long, straight ball only by accident.

To hit such a ball consistently the downswing must be what is commonly known as "inside out." It is the swing of every low-handicap golfer, and it must be yours if you are to cut down your score.

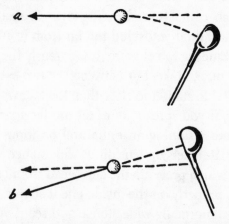

Fig. 10. *Here is shown the difference between* inside out *and* outside in. *In* (a) *the club head is approaching the ball from inside the line of flight and will send the ball along the solid line. In* (b) *the club head is approaching from the outside, and a crooked shot is certain to follow.*

An "inside-out" swing means, merely, that the club head strikes the ball after approaching it from *inside* the line of flight. If the club head approaches the ball from outside the line, a slice or bad pull will usually result. The club head must go into the ball from the *inside*.

And a word of warning here! Don't try to swing the club head *on* or *along* the line of flight on the backswing, figuring that by so doing you will keep the face of the club always square to the direction line and therefore will neither hook nor slice. It won't work. The swing *must* be from the *inside*.

The swing itself falls naturally into two parts, the backswing and the downswing. The purpose of the backswing is to reach a position from which you can deliver the proper downswing—deliver it easily, naturally, with the maximum power and the minimum of effort. In short, once you are in the correct position at the top of the backswing, it is hard to go wrong. The downswing will almost take care of itself.

We shall now violate the order of logical sequence by showing you, first, the correct position at the top and, second, describing the backswing, or how to get to the top.

The position at the top, from two angles, is shown in Figures 11 and 12.

Observe closely in the illustrations the following points:

1. Much more weight on right foot than on left. Weight supported by whole of right foot, particularly the heel, and by inside of ball and toes of left foot. Left carries only a shade more weight than necessary to sustain balance.
2. Hips turned about 45 degrees.

3. Shoulders turned 90 degrees.
4. Right elbow pointing down.
5. Head fixed. No sway, either right or left. No dip, no rise.
6. Left arm reasonably straight but elbow not locked.
7. Left hand grip firm; no loose fingers.
8. Right wrist under shaft.
9. Club still held between thumb and index finger of right hand.
10. Hands even with top of head.
11. Club shaft pointing *across* direction line.
12. Club face half closed.

All these points, in one way or another, are necessary to observe for a single reason: To bring the club head to the ball from the *inside out* with the club face square to the line of flight.

All twelve points are important, but four of them are vital. These are points 1, 5, 8 and 11.

If you can reach the top of the backswing with most of your weight on the right foot, without having moved your head—up, down, or laterally—and if you then have the shaft of the club pointing *across* the line of flight with the right wrist under the shaft, you have taken four tremendous steps toward better golf. You will then be in an excellent position to hit from the inside out.

Let's examine these four points further.

Having most of the weight on the right foot at the top facilitates the correct transfer of weight on the downswing. On the backswing the weight goes from left to right, and on the downswing from right to left. If it doesn't do this the swing will be spoiled, even if everything else is correct.

Fig. 11.   *Figures 11 and 12 are among the most important in the
book, for they show the correct position at the top. In these two
illustrations we can check all 12 points which must be observed.
This front view shows most of the weight on the right foot, the hips
turned 45 degrees, shoulders turned 90 degrees, head fixed, left arm
straight and firm, hands as high as top of head, and thumb and forefinger of right hand gripping club. These are 7 of the 12 points.*

Fig. 12. Here is the top of the backswing from a side view. And here are the other five points: Right elbow pointing down, right wrist under shaft, left-hand grip firm, shaft pointing across the line of flight, and club face half closed.

Wrong weight transference is one of the worst sins of golf and there is no way to atone for it. If the weight is on the right at the top, moving it to the left as the downswing starts is natural and easy, and as the hips make a lateral movement to the left, as well as a turning motion, they move out of the way of the hands. The hands, then, come naturally straight down from the top and swing the club from the inside out. But if the weight is on the left foot at the top, it will invariably shift sharply to the right on the downswing. As it does so it moves the axis of the swing to the right and throws the right hip toward the front. Thus the right hip and right side don't get "out of the way" of the hands. They throw the hands outside and the swing then is made from the outside in.

The importance of correct weight transference cannot be stressed too strongly.

By not moving the head we mean, of course, not moving the body either. The fixed head is supposed to keep the body fixed also. The natural inclination on the backswing is to sway the body to the right, away from the ball. But as soon as you do that you move the center of the swing. It is like moving the hub of the wheel. To get the center of the swing— the hub—back into the correct position you have to sway back to the left on the downswing. In other words, one sway has to counteract another sway. And why have two sways? Why have any at all? They simply complicate the swing. It is much simpler without any sways.

Now, as to the club pointing across the line of flight. This probably surprises you. Yet that is where it should be. True,

you will find many top-flight professionals who do not have
the club pointing across; they will have it parallel to the line
of flight. But these fellows, you will find, do not take quite
the full pivot, compensating for it in another way. But why
should you go in for compensations? You have enough to do
without them.

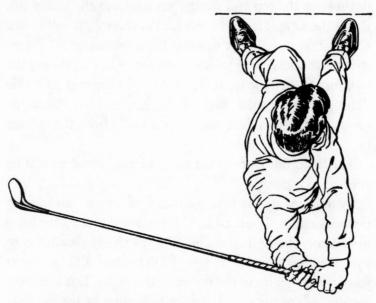

Fig. 13. *Here is the top of the backswing from an overhead angle.
This shows even more clearly what is meant when we say the shaft
should point* across *the direction line.*

The body, which is the axis of the swing, turns through a
much shorter radius than the club head, which is the cir-
cumference of the swing. If, therefore, the club at the top
is only parallel with, or pointing away from, the line of flight,

the turn of the body on the downswing will throw the club head outside the line before it reaches the ball. You want it inside, not outside.

As to the right wrist being under the shaft, well, you will have trouble if it isn't. The right wrist under the shaft means that the right hand is bent backward. When it is, it weakens the grip of the fingers of the right hand, the strong fingers of the strong hand. If that hand and those fingers are in command at the top, the swing is virtually ruined right there. They will most certainly overpower the weaker left hand on the way down and throw the club head outside the line of flight.

For years we were taught to have the left wrist under the shaft at the top. Forget that. When the left wrist is under the shaft, the left hand is bent backward and the fingers of the weaker left hand are loosened on the club, which only insures their being overpowered by the stronger right on the way down. Why weaken the fingers of the hand that already is the weaker of the two? Especially when that hand must be the dominating hand in the swing.

When the right wrist is under the shaft, the line formed by the left wrist and the back of the left hand will be virtually straight at the top. If the left wrist is under the shaft at the top, there will be a sharp angle between the line of the wrist and the back of the left hand. Try that and see for yourself. And don't permit any such angle.

If the left wrist is under the shaft, it will tend to open the club face at the top. But you don't want an open club face. It should be half closed.

Fig. 14. *The position of the wrists is the important thing here. Notice that the right wrist, not the left, is under the shaft. That the right hand is bent back, not the left. Left arm and back of left hand form a straight line. Note, too, that the club face is half closed. If the left hand were bent back, with the left wrist under the shaft, club face would be open.*

There have been great golfers who have swung with a completely closed face at the top. However, they are greatly in the minority, and they were forced to compensate for the closed face by a slight roll of the wrists to the right on the downswing. Without this roll they would have come into the ball with a sharply closed or even hooded club face that would produce a hook or a smother on every shot.

Why, though, should the average golfer make the game more difficult for himself? Most of us have troubles enough without deliberately setting up some action in the swing for which we must later compensate. The fewer things we have to do in the golf swing, the better for all of us.

So, don't try for a completely closed or a completely open face at the top. If it is half closed it is ideal. From that position it will come into the ball neither open nor closed but squarely at right angles to the line of flight. No compensations will be needed. Let's do it the easy way.

Failure to hit from the inside out is the most common fault in golf. To it can be traced at least 95 per cent of the ills of the average player. An inside-out swing is an absolutely indispensable factor in hitting a ball consistently straight and far. It is the one thing that *must* be done. Yet it is the one thing that the chap who is trying to break 90, 100, or 110, consistently fails to do.

Why does he fail? Because he never is in a position at the top of his backswing to hit from the inside out. Usually he is in a position to hit the ball from any other angle, and any other angle produces the shot he doesn't want—usually that slice or that smothered pull that winds up in the tall grass.

THE BACKSWING

Now let's start with a ball teed up in front of us and go about reaching that correct position at the top of the swing that will enable us to hit from the inside out.

With the grip and stance described in the previous chapter we are ready to go about our business. The very first move we make is a critical one. We have been told, and we know from experience, that there are many ways of starting the backswing. We can start it with a turning motion of the left hip, with the hands, with a turn of the left shoulder, with a pushing back of the left hand, with a lateral movement of the hips, with a drag back of the hands, with a slight pushing movement off the ball of the left foot, etc.

Forget all that.

Start the backswing with a turning movement of the body, a turning movement as though the body were *all in one piece*. In other words, as though the arms were welded to their sockets in the shoulders, as if the wrists were incapable of bending, and the fingers unable to yield. This turning movement is coupled with a *slight lateral movement* of the hips from left to right. This lateral movement is important because it facilitates the transfer of weight to the right leg, where it must be as the backswing is carried to the top.

Then, as you turn the body, the arms, wrists, hands, and club will turn with the body as the spokes and the rim of a wheel turn with the hub.

All in one piece. Is the idea clear?

Fig. 15. Here is the beginning of the backswing, showing the all-in-one-piece movement. Body, arms, hands, and club all are going back together. Visible also is the slight lateral shift of the hips to the player's right and the definite transference of weight to the right leg. Study this. It's important.

If you start the backswing this way, with the *slight* lateral movement of the hips, you will find that the club head is brought straight back from the ball for about 12 inches, that the weight has been transferred to the right leg, and that the swing from there on will be definitely *inside* the line of flight. This is very important because it is the beginning of the proper swing, the first step on the path that will bring you to the top of the backswing in position to hit from the inside out.

Now, from that first turn, you simply continue to turn until your shoulders, rotating in an almost horizontal plane, are at right angles to the line of flight. As the turn takes place the weight will shift to the right until, at the top, most of it will be on the right foot, especially the heel. The left heel will have left the ground and only the inside of the ball of the left foot and the big toe will be supporting any weight. And it will support *only a shade more than is necessary to maintain balance.*

There is a slight lateral motion of the hips, from left to right, as they turn, and the trick is for the hips to move and turn *without the head moving laterally with them.* This would be a sway, which we must guard against. And it can be done. It takes practice, but it can be done.

As this turn takes places the hands are raised until they are head high. Before they get this high you will find that the club has reached and passed a vertical position and is dropping down. Before it passes the vertical position it forces the wrists to bend. This bending is called a "break" or a "cock." This bending is correct. In connection with it, however, it is important not to let the wrists bend too soon. Keep them straight in the backswing until the club forces them to

Fig. 16. This shows a continuation of the backswing, with body, arms, hands, and club still moving in one piece. Notice especially that the wrists have not yet begun to break, despite the fact that the body is turned well around. A late break of the wrists is necessary to reach the top in the correct position. Observe too that even more of the weight is on the right leg than in Fig. 15 and that the left heel is off the ground. This is a perfect illustration of how early in the swing the weight moves over to the right leg.

bend. This point will come when your left arm is about parallel to the ground.

Now, after the wrist "break," as the shoulder turn is continued slightly, the club will drop down to a position not farther than parallel to the ground and pointing *across the line of flight.*

This is the top of the backswing. If the other points have been observed, if the head has remained fixed, if the grip of the hands has remained firm, and if most of your weight has moved naturally to your right foot, you are in the right position at the top.

From here, from this position, it will be easy to hit the ball from an inside line. Look back at the illustrations showing the top of the swing. Aren't you in perfect position to hit from the inside out?

Some of these movements and some of the positions described will feel strange to you when you try them or get into the positions. They would. So would your usual faulty positions feel strange and strained to Byron Nelson, Sam Snead, or any other top-flight professional. But you'll quickly become accustomed to the correct position just as you have to the incorrect.

You may have a little trouble with one or two things while you make the turn all in one piece. One is keeping your head fixed. Without a doubt you *think* now that you keep it fixed. But the chances are you don't or you wouldn't be having so much trouble.

So here is a little test. Take a pillow, preferably when your wife is downstairs so she will not think you are completely crazy. Stand close to a wall, facing it, and take your stance but without a club. Place the pillow between the wall and your head. Don't lean against the pillow but stand close enough to the wall so that as you take your normal stance there will be just enough pressure to keep the pillow from dropping.

Now take your backswing. Does the pillow fall? If you are swaying, raising, ducking, or pulling away on your backswing, it will fall or at least move from its position.

But if your head remains fixed through the swing, you will have no trouble with the pillow. Your head will hold it naturally.

This is not only a test. It is an excellent exercise, something you can practice at your leisure, and, even better, something that will show you instantly what we mean by saying: "Keep your head fixed."

The great temptation when you start the swing all in one piece, with the left side as the axis, is to sway to the right. You may be absolutely certain in your own mind that you are not swaying, but unless you watch yourself with extreme care you will sway. It is almost automatic.

That sway you must guard against at all costs. If you sway to the right as you start the backswing, you move the axis to the right, and will only have to bring it back by swaying to the left on the downswing. And what is equally bad, you may either swing the club in too upright a plane or too flat a plane. Either one gives you a bad position at the top from which it is impossible to deliver a correct downswing.

With too upright a swing you are liable to hit from the outside in, and with too flat a swing you will hit with a closed club face. One is about as bad as the other.

Try this. Sway deliberately and see what kind of plane your swing takes, if it's too upright or too flat.

You can test this easily. In the correct plane the hands should be as high as the top of the head. If they are higher the plane is too upright. If they are lower it's too flat.

Now try the backswing *all in one piece* but *without* swaying and see how the club is virtually forced into the right position.

The necessity of fighting this tendency to sway can't be stressed too strongly.

Once you get the idea of swinging all in one piece around the head as a point, without swaying, you have made big strides toward that 89 you are after—or even that 79.

Another tendency in many golfers is to drop or dip the left shoulder on the backswing. Don't fall into that habit. The shoulders should turn in an almost horizontal plane. If the left shoulder dips, it will keep more weight on the left leg than should be there at the top and the left foot will tend to remain flat on the ground. Then when the downswing begins, this weight will flow to the right instead of to the left and the arc of the swing will be thrown outside.

You will find, by taking a few short backswings, that by keeping this left shoulder up you will almost force the weight to move to the right and the left heel to come up off the ground. And you will find, too, that by deliberately dipping that shoulder, you will keep a lot of weight on the left and the left heel on the ground. Try it and see for yourself.

Only in the downswing, when the hands reach the hitting area, do the shoulders get far out of their horizontal plane. At that point the left shoulder definitely rises and the right shoulder passes underneath.

But on the backswing, don't let that left shoulder drop.

Here is another point you can watch. The chances are that you have no idea which way your club points at the top of the swing. If it ever occurred to you to find out, you probably have had someone tell you. But you can see for yourself, and easily.

Take a floor lamp or table lamp. Place it at one side of a room in which you have space to take a full swing with a club. Turn out all lights but this one. Stand with the lamp at your left and swing the club as though you were aiming to send the ball in the direction of the lamp. You will find that the lamp throws your shadow on the opposite wall.

Now swing and stop at the top. Take a peek at the shadow. Is your club pointing away from the direction line, parallel with it, or across it? If it is pointing anywhere but across it, your position at the top is wrong. Get the club pointing across. Once you get it there you will also get the *feel* of the correct position, and you will realize then how easy it will be from there to hit the ball from the inside out.

We mentioned earlier that faulty weight transference is one of the game's worst mistakes. Too many players have too much weight on the left foot at the top and too much on the right foot at impact. Here's how you can check yourself.

If the weight is being transferred properly on the backswing, the left foot should roll to the inside, and at the top the heel should be definitely off the ground. If it isn't, the weight hasn't been moved properly. Again, when the hands reach the hitting area the weight should have been moved to the left leg, the right foot should have rolled to the inside,

Fig. 17. Vitally important is this, the first movement of the down-swing. With reverse hip-turn weight has gone back quickly to left leg. Of equal importance, arms and club have been brought down from top with wrist-cock still retained; there has been no "throw" of the club from the top. Shoulders haven't returned to address position yet, though hips have. Compare this picture with Fig. 11 to see what has been accomplished by first movement of downswing.

and the right heel should have come off the ground slightly.
If you are flat-footed at either point—at the top or at impact
—your weight is moving improperly.

If you have someone watch you at these two points or
take pictures with a fast-action camera, you will know exactly what you are doing.

There is a way by which you can find, for yourself, the
correct position at the top. It is by retracing the downswing
—backward—and it is done this way:

Start from the position you would be in if the clubhead
had hit the ball and gone on about three feet. In this position the head is still over the spot where the ball had been,
both arms are straight, fully extended, the weight is almost
all on the straight left leg, the right knee is bent, the right
heel is off the ground, only the inside of the ball of the right
foot is touching the ground, and the clubhead is directly over
the correct line of flight.

Now, from this position simply *swing the club back,*
through the spot where the ball had been, and right on
back to the top. Don't try to think how it should be
done. Just swing it back. Then hold it, and have someone
show you where the club is, or look in a full length mirror.

The chances are that your backswing will seem flat to you.
You also will find that you didn't use your wrists until you
had almost reached the top. You will discover the right elbow tucked in pretty close to the side. And, finally, you will
find that overswinging is almost impossible with this retracing movement. The latter especially will be true if you

are one of those loose-jointed upright swingers whose club dips well below the horizontal at the top.

This retracing swing is of great value, for it can give to every player the feel of the correct position at the top.

THE DOWNSWING

From the correct position at the top, the downswing is one of the easiest things in all golf.

There is only one special movement to be made and, while this is a vital one, it also is a perfectly natural one. It is this:

From the top of the backswing, turn the hips back to the position they were in at the address, *without any swinging movement of the shoulders, arms, wrists or hands.*

This reverse turn of the hips is much quicker, of course, than the first turn, from left to right on the backswing and it is accompanied by a slight lateral shift of the hips from right to left, because there was a slight shift from left to right on the backswing. Actually this turn and shift will take the hips somewhat to the left of their position at address. But only a little. Don't try to swing them way around to the left. That will only throw shoulders, hands and club outside the line.

The important thing is that the hips must lead.

The reverse hip-turn performs this vitally important function:

It transfers the weight from the right leg and foot, to the left, where it must be. The weight on the left leg, before the club is swung through, has the effect of stiffening the left side and relaxing the right. The stiffened left side, carrying the weight, gives the player something to "hit against," and the relaxed right side clears the way for the right shoulder and hands to come down and through on the inside and thus deliver an inside-out blow with the club.

We mentioned earlier that this first movement, the reverse hip-turn, was a natural one. It is because, if you are in the correct position at the top, the weight is on the right leg. The only direction you can move, then, is to the left, unless you fall down. The only time this correct weight transference is difficult and unnatural is when you have too much weight on the left foot at the top. Remember that.

So much for the hips. Let's turn now to the rest of the action in the downswing.

We have said that the reverse hip-turn should be made without any swinging motion of the shoulders, arms, wrists or hands. This is extremely important. It is necessary to prevent hitting too soon.

You will find that when the hips go back to and beyond their address position, without any swinging motion of the rest of the body, their turning movement alone will bring the shoulders almost around to their address position, and the arms and club part way down. The turning action of the shoulders on the downswing is in a more vertical plane, whereas they turn *almost* horizontally on the backswing.

The word *almost* is italicized because it is important that in this first movement of the downswing the shoulders do not return all the way to their position at address. When the hands and arms go to work in the second movement of the downswing the shoulders will complete their turn—*but not until then.* The hips will have turned to the left of the ball but not the shoulders. They will be still turned slightly to the right of the ball, certainly no more than square to it. A line drawn through the shoulders at this stage would not yet be quite parallel to the direction line.

The shoulders, in a large part, control the direction of the swing, their position determining whether it will be inside out or outside in. If, after the reverse hip turn, the shoulders face to the left of the ball, the swing will be from the outside in. But if they face to the right of the ball, or no more than directly toward it, the swing will be from the inside out. You can see this for yourself by taking a few practice swings with the shoulders in the positions mentioned.

How, you may ask, is this correct shoulder action to be accomplished?

All you need do is make the reverse shoulder-turn in more of a vertical plane, and *keep the head fixed.* If the head stays back, then the shoulders will not turn too far around. It's as simple as that. If you keep the head back, and fixed, the shoulders will take care of themselves.

As the hips go back to the left, they will bring the straight left arm down until it is virtually parallel to the ground. But since the wrists have made no movement of their own the angle of the wrist-cock still is the same as it was at the top. As a consequence, the shaft of the club will not quite yet have reached a vertical position.

This is the beginning of the downswing. Try it yourself by going to the top, turning the hips back to their address position, and then stopping. See where your left arm is. See that it is parallel to the ground and that the club is not quite yet in a vertical position. See that the shoulders have returned to no more than a "square to the ball" position, perhaps not quite that much. Notice that most of your weight now is on your left foot, and that that foot is planted firmly on the ground. It should be there.

With the hip-turn, the arms, wrists, hands and club are brought down half way from the top *all in one piece.* You may recall that in the backswing these arms, wrists, hands and club were taken back all in one piece by the body turn. The movement on the downswing is not quite the same, but almost. The hips turn first in the downswing and the rest follow. But the rest follow *all in one piece.* The rest are *pulled down* by the action of the hips but they still are in *one piece.* There is no shoulder, arm, wrist or hand action in it.

From this halfway-down position, the arms, wrists and hands go to work. They have all the power stored up by the wrist-cock and they are in a perfect position to hit from the inside out. From there they can't hit too soon and they can't hit from the outside. They can hit as hard, then, as they want to.

Of course, these two actions—the hip-turn to the left and the arm and hand action—flow into each other so smoothly and swiftly that you don't see them separately when you watch a golfer swing. The slow-motion picture camera catches them, though, beautifully. The camera will prove they take place, if you happen to doubt it.

Where the struggling golfer runs into trouble is starting the downswing with his shoulders, arms and hands and following with the hip-turn, or in making both at the same time.

It should be quite obvious that if you start to swing the club with your arms and hands right from the top, you will exhaust the power stored up by the wrist-cock long before the clubhead reaches the ball. When the club reaches the hitting area, when it should be traveling at its greatest speed, you will have nothing left to hit with. If you hit the ball, then, it won't go very far.

So get the correct habits thoroughly ingrained. Develop them by practice swings, starting down with the hip turn and stopping, to check the position of the left arm, the shoulders and the shaft of the club.

A factor which can speedily wreck this correct sequence of movements is anxiety, which causes a speeding up of the whole swing. If you get in a big enough hurry to hit the ball, you'll start from the top with your hands instead of your hips. That will lead only to disaster.

Take it smoothly and easily. Don't rush it, ever.

PART TWO

The Nine Bad Shots
And What Causes Them

SLICING: *Hitting with an open face, usually from the outside in*

HOOKING: *Hitting with a shut face*

TOPPING: *Hitting with a lifted head, a sway to the right, or hitting with a raised arc*

SMOTHERING: *Hitting with club face hooded*

PULLING: *Hitting from the outside in with a shut face*

PUSHING: *Hitting with an open face while the club is still moving from the inside out*

SKYING: *Hitting with a chopping downswing, usually with a sway to the left or with the club face turned over*

SCLAFFING: *Hitting with too much weight on the right foot*

SHANKING: *Hitting with little or no pivot, very loose wrists, and with an exaggerated outside-in swing*

CHAPTER THREE

SLICING

HERE IS the most common fault in golf beyond the shadow of a doubt.

At a conservative guess, 90 per cent of the people who take up the game quickly become chronic slicers unless they are caught in time by expert instruction. You could almost say they are "natural" slicers.

Some few, afflicted early by the malady and unable to make any headway against it, actually give up the game. Most, though, struggle along with it, fighting it continually, and often bringing it under something that passes for control. You've all played with the fellow who knows he will slice every shot, is resigned to it, and allows for it by aiming everything to the left. When the expected curve to the right materializes, this chap is right in the middle of the fairway. Not very far, of course, but safe. He doesn't expect to break 90 or even 100. On those days when the slice doesn't come off he's in bad shape.

Then there's the long hitter with the slice. He's inherently a better player and often hits a long, straight ball. But he seldom scores as well as he "should" because that slice will break out suddenly, and he'll have three or four bad holes to spoil his card. This type of player can be extremely wild on his bad days. He pulls as well as slices so he is off the fairway on both sides, and with his length he can get very deep in that spinach. On his good days he's around in fairly respectable figures. But he's never very happy because he never knows when that slice will strike him down.

What is at the root of all this evil?

The answer is: Hitting the ball with a club face that is open at impact.

Fig. 18.   Here is the contact for a sliced shot. The club face is open. The dotted line shows where it should be, square to the direction line.

This is true regardless of whether the path of the club is inside out or outside in, with one exception. This exception is the push, the straight ball to the right of the target that occurs when the body sways ahead of the ball and is accompanied by an inside-out swing and a slightly open club face. In this one exception the club face, although open so far as the direction line is concerned, is square to the direction in which the club head is traveling, thereby producing a straight ball to the right.

But that will interest you only if you are pushing a lot of shots. If you are slicing you won't be pushing, so forget about it.

A slice occurs when the club head is traveling directly along the direction line at the moment of impact or when it is traveling from the outside in.

In the former the ball goes out straight along the direction line because the force has been applied in that direction, but the open club face gives it a left-to-right spin. This causes it, eventually, to curve to the right. This is the tail-end slice, which is more of a fade and doesn't cause too much trouble.

In the latter case, when the blow is delivered with an outside-in swing, the ball starts to the left and then curves to the right. The force has been applied from the outside, that is, from right to left, which causes the ball to start to the left. But the spin given by the open face produces the curve to the right.

This is the killer, the slice of most golfers; this is the one that drives them to distraction and nineteenth-hole vows never to pick up a club again. It's probably the one that's bothering you, so that's the one we'll go after.

In attacking this slice there are, obviously, two points to hit and eliminate. One is the open face at impact, the other is the outside-in swing.

THE OPEN FACE

A face that is open at impact was also open at the top of the backswing. You can be sure of that. So, in setting out to get rid of that open face, first check your grip. An open face at the top comes either from a wrong grip or a wrong position of the hands at the top.

Bad Grip

Take the grip first. Be sure that the knuckles of at least three fingers of the left hand can be seen as you address the ball. If less than three can be seen then your left hand is too far to the left on the shaft of the club. If it is too far to the left it will produce, without ever failing, an open face at the top. Try this for yourself and prove it.

Take a grip with the left hand that shows less than three knuckles, and place the right hand on the shaft so that the V formed by the thumb and forefinger point straight up or to the left shoulder.

Now swing back and see whether the face is open or closed at the top. It will be open. You can bet on it. If it isn't wide open it will be much more open than it should be.

It should be *half closed.*

The face opens at the top and at impact with this wrong grip for the simple reason that in taking it the left wrist is

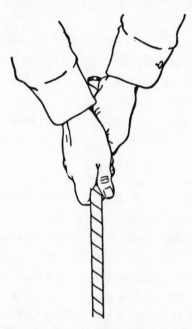

Fig. 19. *A grip like this always will produce an open face at the top and an open face at contact. The V formed by the thumb and forefinger of the right hand points straight up instead of to the right shoulder. The grip of the left hand is far too much to the player's left.*

turned slightly to the left. It is turned slightly out of a nattural position. It will be strained just a trifle. As soon as it starts to work or move, that left wrist returns to an unstrained position. In this case that means it will turn slightly to the right. As soon as it does this, it opens the face of the club. You can prove that to yourself, too, by taking the wrong grip, twisting your left wrist to the right, and watching the club face open, even while it rests on the ground.

If the V formed by the thumb and forefinger of the right hand, for instance, point directly up rather than to the right shoulder, the right hand is in a wrong position. Move it somewhat to the right.

So much for the grip causing an open face.

Wrong Position at Top of Swing

The other reason for the open face, as mentioned, is a wrong position of the hands at the top.

If, with the correct grip, you reach the top with the left wrist under the shaft, you will open the face of the club. You will have to strain a little to do it but it can be done. In fact many a golfer has made a point of getting that left wrist under the shaft because he has read in golf books that that is where it should be.

It should *not* be there.

The *right* wrist should be under the shaft.

When the right wrist is under, the club face will be half closed *if the grip is correct.*

Possibly the only way you can convince yourself of this is to show it to yourself. So take the correct grip. Go to the top of the backswing and hold it. Now put the left wrist under the shaft. See the face open? Now put the right wrist under

Fig. 20. One of the game's worst sins is pictured here—a loose grip with the left hand at the top and with the left wrist bent under the shaft. The club face, as you see, is wide open. The dotted line shows where it would be if it were half closed. Never let that left hand open.

and see the difference. The face is half closed, isn't it? If your grip is correct it will be.

And that is the story on the open face. If you are slicing, track down those two causes of opening the face and you will find that one or the other will be at the root of it.

FROM THE OUTSIDE IN

Now for the other cause of slicing: Hitting from the outside in.

If a golfer hits the ball while his club head is traveling from the outside to the inside of the direction line, he can be absolutely certain that

1. He never was in a completely correct position at the top of the backswing, or
2. He threw the club with his hands from the top.

The right position at the top has been described carefully and fully in the chapter on The Swing. But for the sake of clarity we will list again the 12 main points to be observed at the top.

1. Much more weight on right foot than on left. Left carries only enough to sustain balance.
2. Hips turned about 45 degrees.
3. Shoulders turned 90 degrees.
4. Right elbow pointing down.
5. Head fixed. No sway.
6. Left arm reasonably straight.
7. Left hand grip firm; no loose fingers.
8. Right wrist under shaft.
9. Club still held by thumb and index finger of right hand.
10. Hands even with top of head.
11. Club shaft pointing *across* line of flight.
12. Club face half closed.

The only job, then, is reaching the correct position at the top. And this is not hard if the correct grip is taken and instructions on the backswing are followed. They will lead you to the right position at the top with only a little effort and practice.

To check yourself on these 12 points you will need a

friend to watch you—a friend who knows what the 12 points are and exactly what to look for.

Let's go over those points briefly inasmuch as they already have been covered in the chapter on The Swing. We'll discuss them only as they affect an outside-in swing.

1. If the weight is on the right foot at the top, it will go to the left as the hip-turn is made to start the downswing. There is a lateral movement of the hips at this point, from right to left. This movement, in a sense, takes the hips "out of the way" and permits the hands to start straight down from the top, thereby bringing the club down on the inside. But if the weight is mostly on the left foot at the top, it will shift to the right as the downswing starts. This throws the center of the swing to the right and throws the right hip out toward the front. The whole right side, including the hands, is forced toward the front with the hip, and the hands and club are thrown outside. The rest of the swing then is from the outside in.

Dipping the left shoulder on the backswing will tend to prevent the correct transference of weight. If the shoulders rotate evenly, on a horizontal plane, the weight will be carried to the right much more easily.

2. If the hips don't turn on the backswing the player will find it almost impossible to turn his shoulders a full 90 degrees. If this full turn, this pivot, isn't made, the shaft won't point *across* the line of flight at the top and the first movement of the downswing will throw the club outside.

3. If the shoulders are not turned 90 degrees from the address position, they will turn back too quickly and too far as

Fig. 21.   From a position at the top like this you could hardly do
anything but slice or shank. Everything is wrong. There is too much
weight on the left leg, neither hips nor shoulders have turned
enough, the left arm and left hand are loose, the left wrist is under
the shaft, the right elbow points out to the rear, the club face is
open, and shaft is pointing away from the direction line. But this is
a common position. Compare it with Figs. 11 and 12.

the hip turn is made on the downswing and thus throw the club outside. With a full 90-degree turn they make it easy to bring the club down on the inside.

4. A right elbow that sticks out from the side like the wing of a bird in flight spells right-hand domination because it indicates the right wrist is not in its correct position under the shaft.

5. If the head is fixed, the club will be swung around a fixed axis and can be swung from the inside out easily. A sway to the right on the backswing moves the axis to the right, and in order to hit from the inside out the axis must be swayed back again to the address position before impact.

6. If the left arm is not reasonably straight, the radius of the swing will have been shortened from what it was at address. You'll simply have to straighten out the elbow and regain the full radius sometime before you hit the ball. But this is needless. Harry Vardon did it, we admit. But who among us is a Vardon? And why set up a couple of extra motions in a swing that gives you enough trouble now?

7. Unless your left hand has a firm grip it is liable—almost certain—to be overpowered by the right hand. Right-hand domination from the top leads inevitably to throwing the club outside the line early in the downswing or closing the face—or both.

8. When the right wrist is under the shaft, it means that the right hand is bent back and weakened as it should be. If the right wrist is not under, the left wrist will be. And when the left wrist is under, it means that the weaker left hand has been weakened still more by being bent backward

and that the stronger right hand has been strengthened. This can only mean that the right hand will take charge early in the downswing and throw the club outside.

9. If the club drops between the right thumb and forefinger at the top, control has been lost to some extent. Any loss of control tends to throw the club outside.

10. If the hands are even with the top of the head at the top of the backswing it is a sure indication the swing is neither too flat nor too upright. If they are below the head, level with the neck for instance, the swing is too flat. If they are above the head, it's too upright.

11. If the club is not pointing *across* the line of flight, the first motion of the downswing (the hip turn), will be liable to throw it outside. If it is pointing across, then the hip turn will still bring it down on the inside.

12. The open and closed club face has been gone into thoroughly. Suffice it to say that an open face at the top brings an open face at impact and thereby promotes slicing.

HITTING FROM THE TOP

Hitting too soon, which is only another phrase for hitting from the top, is insidious as well as destructive. It is also tied in so closely with the correct position at the top and with the first movement of the downswing that treating it separately is almost impossible.

If the position at the top of the backswing is wholly correct, there will be no tendency to hit from the top. But if the weight has not been transferred correctly, or if the left wrist is under the shaft, or if the hands loosen their grip even the slightest, the player will hit too soon. Unconsciously but invariably he will throw the club right from the top. By the time his hands get down to his hips, the club shaft and his left arm will form virtually a straight line. He will already have delivered his blow, his power will be gone and he will not yet have hit the ball. When the hands are hip high on the downswing, the club shaft should not yet have reached a horizontal position.

So if you are hitting from the top the place to look for the reason is almost always in your position at the top. Check it most carefully, with the help of a friend who knows what to look for.

The only other place to look is in the first movement of the downswing. Once you are certain that your position at the top is correct, make sure that your next movement is with your hips. Make the reverse hip turn first. Then—and only then—let the arms and hands bring the club down to the ball. Deliberately hold the hands back, if necessary, but be sure you make that hip turn first.

AM I SWINGING FROM THE OUTSIDE?

In trying to correct your slice it would be natural, perhaps, for you to wonder whether you actually are hitting from the outside or not. Or maybe you are a chap who has to be shown anyway. Well, you can show yourself. Without anyone helping you, you can make the test and supply your own proof.

Tee up a ball. Now stick another tee into the ground

about 5 inches to the left of the ball and 3½ inches inside the direction line. Now hit the ball.

If your swing is from the inside out, the second tee will be undisturbed.

But if you are hitting from the outside in, you will not only hit the ball but you also will knock the second tee out of the ground.

The following is one other way to tell, without any "props."

Observe the position of your hands at the finish of the swing.

If your hands pull around quickly to the left as you hit the ball and wind up near your left shoulder, you can be certain your swing has been wrong. It has been from the outside in.

But if your hands at the finish follow straight out after the ball, as they will in the correct swing, then you can be sure you have hit from the inside out.

If you are hitting a lot of bad shots and wondering why, watching the position of your hands at the finish will give you a pretty good clue. This may easily show you that you are hitting from the outside, which usually means you have been hitting from the top. Thus you can immediately go about applying the correctives.

Of course, at the complete finish of a correct swing, the hands eventually will be pulled around to the left by the action of the body after they have gone straight out after the ball. Don't be misled by this. They will go straight out first. You can best check the position of your own hands by chok-

Fig. 22. Here is the peg test. Note the tee stuck in the ground and notice that this fellow's outside-in swing (along the solid line) will continue on and knock that peg out of the ground. If his swing were from the inside out, along the dotted line, it would miss the peg. You can use this test with a driver as well as with an iron.

ing off your follow-through, if any. See where they are then.

Another thing. Don't be fooled by pictures of the top professionals showing their hands well around to the left after hitting a shot. Those pictures are posed for the photographers. The pro usually hasn't hit a ball. He's just swinging for the cameraman, and he has to swing through and "hold" his position at the finish so there will be no movement of the club. If the club were moving it would spoil the picture. When he does this his hands sag, his whole body sags, and he is in nothing like the position he'd be in if he actually had hit a ball.

SUMMARY OF CORRECTIONS
FOR SLICING

Check grip. Three knuckles of left hand must show. Both V's must point to right shoulder.

Check club face at top. Must be *half* closed.

Check right wrist at top. Must be under shaft. Left must not be under.

Check left hand at top. Fingers must not be open. Grip must be firm.

Check start of backswing. Must be *all in one piece*, dominated by left side, around head as fixed point.

Check position at top. Shaft must point *across line of flight*, shoulders must have turned 90 degrees, and much more weight must be on right foot than on left.

Check sway. Head must not move.

Check hitting from top. Position of hands at finish will show it.

Check first movement of downswing. If hip turn isn't first move, club may be thrown outside line.

Check throwing hips too far around to left on first movement of downswing. This can throw whole swing outside.

Check dipping left shoulder on backswing. Shoulders must turn on an almost horizontal plane.

Check shoulders on first movement of downswing. Must still be turned slightly to right of ball.

CHAPTER FOUR

HOOKING

WE COME now to a fault that is not among the worst in golf, by any means, and, hence, it is not too common among average players. Of course, to tell a really good player that hooking isn't a bad fault might ruffle him slightly since hooking may be about the only fault he has. Yet it is a fact that the average player, the one who scores from 95 up, isn't bothered much by the shot that curves to the left. Hooking is the good player's error.

The average player will often hit the ball straight to the left, which is a pull, and he may get a few pulled hooks that are accidents. But he virtually never hits a ball that starts straight or a little to the right and then sees it curve to the left. This is because the average player's swing is from the outside in and, therefore, the ball starts to the left instead of straight out, or to the right.

THE CLOSED FACE

The basic cause of hooking is a closed club face at the moment of impact; a face closed, that is, to the direction the club head is following.

If the closing of the club face is slight or moderate, the result will be a hook. If it is so pronounced as to actually reverse the natural loft of the club face, then the ball never will get off the ground and the shot will be what is known as smothered.

Take a club, any club. Lay the club head behind the ball as in the address. Now, having taken your grip, roll your

Fig. 23. Contact with a closed face. The dotted line shows position the club head should be in. This contact will produce either a hook or a smother.

wrists slightly to the left and see what happens to the club head. See it turn? See the toe turn in? See how the toe gets ahead of the heel? And see how the loft of the face is reduced?

You will see also how the angle of the face to the line of

flight is changed. Instead of the face being at right angles to the line of flight, it is at less than right angles. A line drawn perpendicular to the club face now would go to the left of the intended line of flight.

You may ask, perhaps, why the ball would hook. With the club face turned to the left, why wouldn't the ball fly more or less straight to the left of the intended line of flight?

The answer lies in the direction from which the club head approaches the ball, in other words, the direction of force.

If this force is applied from outside the line of flight—an outside-in swing—then the ball would start to the left. Perhaps it would hook moderately and perhaps not at all. It might turn out to be a pull, which is a straight ball to the left of the target. It would be a pull if the face were square to the direction the club head was following.

If the force is applied from directly behind the ball along the line of flight as in the correct inside-out swing, the ball will start straight but the closed club face will cause it to curve to the left.

If the direction of force comes from well inside the line of flight, as it will with a swing that is too much from the inside, the ball will start to the right, but the closed club face will cause it to curve to the left. This will be the biggest hook of all. You've probably seen shots like this occasionally. The ball will start as if it were going out of bounds to the right but will pick up a huge hook and finish in the rough to the left.

Corresponding directions of force, but with the club face open instead of closed, will produce varying degrees of slices.

Regardless of the direction of force, however, we are concerned here chiefly with a closed club face.

A face closed at the moment of striking the ball almost invariably also will be closed at the top of the swing. So our next move will be to go farther back and find what causes a closed club face at the top. (We always work backward in looking for our reasons, as you will notice, like a detective reconstructing a crime.)

A closed face at the top is caused by one or both of two things: (1) a bad grip and/or (2) a bad backswing.

Faulty Grip

If the grip is correct, as we have described it in detail in our chapter on The Grip, then the grip will not cause the face to be closed at the top.

However, if the left hand is too much on top of the shaft (more than three knuckles showing at the address) or if the right hand is too far under the shaft then look out for a face closed too much at the top. Either hand in the wrong position will tend to do it but, unfortunately, when one hand is in the wrong position, the other hand will be too, as a rule.

The reason this faulty grip closes the club face is because it turns the wrists to the right, out of a natural, unstrained position into an unnatural and strained position.

Try it. Address the ball again with the wrong grip we have defined, the left hand well on top of the shaft and the right well under. Now, without loosening your hold on the club, turn the wrists to the left until only three knuckles of the left hand are visible and the V formed by the thumb and fore-finger of the left hand points to the right shoulder.

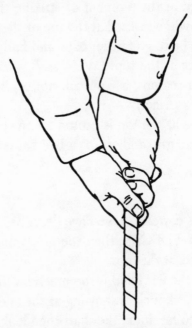

Fig. 24. This is a hook grip. Both hands are much too far to the player's right. Both V's point far outside the right shoulder. Compare this with the correct grip in Fig. 4.

Now look at the club head. The face is definitely closed, isn't it?

That's exactly what happens when you use this incorrect grip. The motion of the wrists turning back to the left into a comfortable, unstrained position takes place on the backswing soon after the club head leaves the ball. When you get to the top of the swing, the wrists are in a normal position but they have turned the club head until the face is closed at the top.

And closed it will remain on the downswing.

Fig. 25. *Here we see the effect of the grip in Fig. 24. The club face is closed tight at the top. You can be dead certain it will be closed at impact too.*

When the face is closed at the top, the only way it can be unclosed, or made normal, at impact is by rolling the wrists to the right on the downswing.

Bad Backswing

Now let's take the faulty backswing that was our second cause for a closed face at the top. The backswing that will do this is one of two types. It is either much too flat or it is a right-hand "pickup."

When a backswing starts too flat but is normal in other respects, it opens the club face quickly and then proceeds to close it just as quickly. And when you get to the top of this very flat swing, you have a face that is closed tight.

Almost invariably the very flat swinger starts the club head away from the ball with a roll of the wrists to the right and swings the club around his waist like a batter in baseball. When he does this he, perforce, has to roll those wrists back to the left on the downswing, and the chances are 100 to 1 that he'll roll them too much and close the face at impact.

But if he starts his backswing *all in one piece*, as in the chapter on The Swing, he won't roll his wrists, he won't be too flat, and the club face will not be closed either at the top or at impact.

The right-hand "pickup" is quite a common fault. We have spoken often, and will continue to do so, of right-hand domination at the top of the swing and of the right hand taking control on the downswing. Well, the "pickup" is worse than that. It is right-hand domination at the very start. And thereby it kills every possibility of a good shot.

This fault is exactly what its name implies. The right hand picks up the club head from behind the ball and slings it

Fig. 26. *A flat backswing. Here again the club face is closed at the top, and when this fellow makes his reverse hip turn he probably will throw the club outside and either hook badly or smother.*

over the right shoulder somewhere—anywhere. When it does, the club face will be closed tight at the top.

The "pickup" comes from several things, chief of which are a complete lack of confidence and an equally complete ignorance of what the golf swing should be.

If we go back to our chapter on The Swing and follow the movements of it even approximately, there will not be a tendency to pick up the club with the right. The very thought of starting the backswing *all in one piece* with the *left side* dominating will kill any "pickup" quickly and thoroughly.

One other fact about hooking, which must be obvious to everyone: The right hand is gripping the club more tightly than the left, at address. The left hand always should grip slightly more firmly than the right, because the left is the one that is to dominate and guide the swing, not the right. But the point here is that, if you have the combination palm-and-finger grip with your left hand, and the finger grip with your right, the left will have a firmer grip. It will have it without the player exerting more pressure with the left. This is because the partial palm grip gives the left more strength. Obviously there is more strength in the palm of your hand than in the fingers alone. So, with the palm and finger grip, and equal pressure applied by both hands, the left will have the stronger grip. Thus you see how the correct grip takes care of left-hand firmness for you—does it automatically.

In addition to the wrong grip and faulty backswing, there is one other factor that can cause a hook. That is our old

Fig. 27. A quick lift, with an equally fast wrist break, are shown vividly in this picture. The player is also beginning to dip his left side slightly, with too much weight retained on the left leg. Dotted lines show where the club should be at this point.

enemy, right-hand domination on the downswing, the same thing that causes a slice, a smother, and a pull.

If the position of the hands at the top is bad; that is to say, if the left wrist is under the shaft and the weaker left hand thereby further weakened, you may hook as well as commit one of the other deadly sins. For then the stronger right will take charge on the downswing and, in addition to throwing the club head outside the line for an outside-in swing, it may also roll the wrists slightly. If it does, then you will get a pulled hook or a pulled smother. So be dead certain that your left hand is strong and in the correct position—not under the shaft—at the top of the swing.

SUMMARY OF CORRECTIONS FOR HOOK

Check grip. Left hand may be too much on top of shaft and right may be too far under. Be sure of correct grip.

Check for fully closed face at top of backswing. Should be *half* closed.

Check position of hands at top. Be sure right wrist is under shaft and that left hand is strong.

Check firmness of grip. Right hand never should grip tighter than left. Left hand should be a little firmer.

Check backswing. May be too flat. See chapter on Swing.

Check right-hand "pickup." Be sure left arm doesn't bend. See chapter on Swing.

Check wrists rolling to right on backswing. Don't roll them. Start backswing *all in one piece* as if arms and wrists had no joints.

CHAPTER FIVE

TOPPING

TOPPING A golf shot is rarely the sin of a golfer with much experience. It is a common fault of the duffer and the veritable bane of the beginner.

True, a good player occasionally tops a shot but it is only occasionally. The chap who scores from 95 down isn't guilty of "skulling" them very often.

No golfer needs to be reminded of the immediate and complete catastrophe that can follow a top. Step on any tee in front of which there is a brook, a pond, a ravine, or a cross bunker to be carried, and the knowledge of what will happen if you top your drive is enough to give any duffer an advanced case of the jitters. The tightening-up that follows has made many an unhappy fellow do exactly what he was trying hardest not to do.

There can be scarcely any argument as to what causes topping. This vile member of the bad-shot family stems from one of three things: jerking the head up, swaying or raising the arc of the swing.

Of course, all three can be combined and all may have to be eliminated (should be eliminated) before the topping can be stopped. The player who finds himself in a fit of topping will have to check himself on all three. Which is the most common is difficult to say, but it doesn't make much difference anyway.

JERKING THE HEAD UP

Let's examine the first cause, jerking the head up. This is commonly known as "looking up." But there is a difference, actually. If we looked up merely by turning the head to the left as we hit the ball, the damage would not be great. Lots of pros and top-flight amateurs do that all the time and it doesn't bother them. The swing has gone so far by the time they take a peek that nothing can change it, and, more important, they merely turn the head without altering the position of the body.

Trouble comes when we jerk our head up and our shoulders up and to the left at the same time. That motion changes the axis of the swing. Lifting the shoulders to which the arms are attached, of course, raises the club that is attached to the arms. Therefore, we top the ball. Reasonable, isn't it?

The cure for all this is a smooth, rhythmic, correct swing.

At this point we differ from the popular conception that it is the lifted head that pulls the shoulders up. We believe that the lifting shoulders throw the head up. If we accept this reasoning, then it follows logically that if the swing itself is smooth and correct, there will be no lifted shoulders and hence no jerked-up head. The best proof that the shoulders throw the head up, and not vice versa, is that the head often comes up without affecting the shoulders, whereas the shoulders never come up without affecting the head.

Now, why do the shoulders come up? In one word, tension. If a player is overanxious, tied up, and tight as he comes

Fig. 28. This is one of the best-known ways to top a shot. The player has failed to keep his head fixed as he swings the club down to the ball. The head has moved to the player's left and up, and with the head have gone the shoulders and upper part of the body. The arc of the swing has been completely destroyed.

through the downswing, the odds are 1,000 to 1 that he has hit from the top, has lost all rhythm, all power he had in his hands and wrists. He has nothing left to hit with. And so he goes into the ball with a heaving, lifting motion of his body, usually his shoulders. This is what causes the shoulders to lift, and with them the head.

We have had pupils with stiff necks and neck and shoulder muscles badly strained from exactly this motion. Once they were straightened out and were swinging smoothly and correctly, they didn't heave their bodies—and they lost their stiff necks.

So, to stop this form of topping we can only recommend that you concentrate on swinging the club correctly and that, when you come to a shot about which you are anxious, you concentrate on swinging smoothly, not on where the ball will go.

Of course, there's a strong possibility that a chronic head lifter doesn't think he looks up and won't believe it if anyone tells him. Golfers can be very stubborn fellows.

If there is any question about whether a player looks up or not, it can be settled quite easily and also convincingly. Try the following:

Have the player who doubts that he looks up tee a ball, take his stance, and address it. Then have a friend (an enemy is just as good) stand on the far side of the ball with his feet just out of range of the club head and facing the player. Let this friend place his right hand lightly but firmly on the player's head. Then let the player swing.

If the player's head pulls away from the friend's hand or

Fig. 29. Here is pictured the test to determine whether or not you sway or lift your head. The player is ready to take a full swing, and if his head moves in any direction, both he and his friend will know it immediately.

turns under the hand, on the downswing the player is looking up. The friend will see it instantly, and the player will know it too. If he is yanking his head up he will feel the friend's hand trying to hold it still.

This is quite a neat trick and will prove to any head lifter that he really moves his head, no matter how obstinate he is in denying it.

SWAYING MOVES THE ARC

Swaying, the second cause of topping, does its deadly work by moving the arc of the swing.

In a correct swing with no sway, the lowest point of the arc the club head makes is right at the ball itself. There is a slight exception to this in the case of iron shots. In these the ball is struck a descending blow. It is struck while the club head still is on the way down, just before it reaches the bottom point of the arc. In wooden-club shots the lowest point of the arc is at the ball.

Now, if you move that whole arc 3 or 4 inches to the right, the lowest point will be a couple of inches behind the ball. Therefore, when the club head reaches the ball it will be starting to rise from its lowest point. As a consequence, it may well strike the ball above the center and therefore top it.

When the player sways to the right on the backswing and does not return on the downswing quite to the point at which he started to sway, he moves the whole axis and arc of the swing to the right. Simple, isn't it?

So the antidote is: Don't sway. If you don't sway you won't move the axis or the arc.

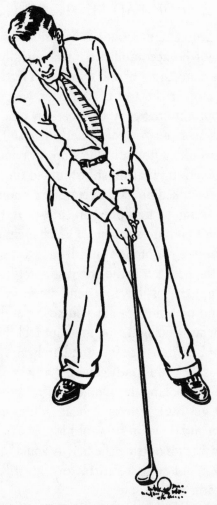

Fig. 30. *This is another way a shot may be topped—by swaying to the right. This player has had too much weight on his left leg at the top of the backswing. As he comes down to the ball, his weight shifts back sharply to his right leg, which throws the low point of the swing's arc behind the ball. The club head is rising at contact and hits the ball on top.*

The next problem, naturally, is how not to sway.

This cannot be accomplished mechanically; it must be done by conscious thought and effort. It is not, for instance, like a shut face at the top of the backswing that can be brought about automatically by a certain type of grip. We wish there were some grip, or something else that could be done, that would automatically stop swaying. But there isn't. It is something that must be worked on by the player himself—and worked on hard over quite a period of time.

The first thing to be done, of course, is to determine whether or not you are swaying. The chances are 100 to 1 that you think you're not. So you will have to test yourself.

Probably the best test is the one just described for detecting looking up; that is, have a friend stand in front of you with one hand on your head as you swing and actually hit a ball. If your sway is slight, you may not feel the pressure of his hand. But he will notice it immediately and will tell you. This test is just as good for discovering a sway as it is to find whether you are looking up. Don't be afraid to use it. Your friend won't get hurt. The club head will swing under his extended arm and down in front of his toes. All he has to do is stand a few inches outside the ball as you address it.

Another test, not quite so satisfactory but still good, is one you can perform by yourself.

Take a club in a room where there is space to swing it. Face a wall on which there are vertical lines. Many types of wallpaper will serve the purpose admirably but you may have to put lines on the wall yourself. It is wiser to do this while your wife is visiting her mother. Now put a strong light directly behind you so that the shadow of your head will be thrown on the wall that has the vertical lines.

Take your stance so that the shadow of the left side of your head touches one of the vertical lines. Be sure which line it is.

Now make your backswing and hold it.

And now look at the wall without moving.

Has the shadow of your head moved? Does the left side of it still touch the same vertical line it touched at the address? If it doesn't, you have definite proof that you are swaying.

If you will continue to swing with your shadow against that wall until you can make your complete swing, or at least your backswing, without having the shadow move, you will be well on the road to eliminating that sway. You will at least feel the difference between swaying and not swaying.

If you do enough of this work with the lamp and the shadow, you will build up the habit of swinging without a sway and you will carry that habit with you out on the course. On the course, incidentally, you can use the sun and your shadow on the ground to check yourself.

So much for discovering a sway to the right and putting a stop to it.

RAISING THE ARC

Now for the third reason for topping—raising the arc of the swing.

This is a common fault of beginners. Actually, the arc is

raised on the backswing so that shoulders, body, and head all are higher at the top of the backswing than they were at the beginning. Naturally, the chap who accomplishes this feat leaves himself no chance to hit the ball squarely. In fact, he is lucky to hit it at all.

This lifting usually comes from one or more of three things: A body bent over too far at address, too much weight on the left leg on the backswing, or straightening the right knee into a locked position at the top of the swing.

In addressing the ball the body should be bent as little as possible. The player should stand straight, bend his knees slightly, and then set the club head behind the ball. Very little bending is required for this—much less than you think.

If a player leans over bending sharply at the waist at the address, he is almost certain to straighten up as he takes the club back. He is equally certain not to return on the downswing to his bent position at address. Once he leaves the bent position the arc of the swing is raised. Rarely can it be lowered precisely to its starting point.

A position that is as erect as possible at the address is the cure.

A second cause for raising the arc is the result of too much weight on the left leg at the top of the swing. This is usually combined with dipping the left knee and left shoulder during the backswing. When most of the weight is on the left leg at the top, the only place for it to go on the downswing is back to the right. When there is a pronounced dip of the left side on the backswing, the tendency on the downswing,

Fig. 31. If you lean and reach for the ball like this at address, you are very likely to straighten up on the backswing and stay up on the downswing. Hence, the arc of the swing is raised and you hit the ball on top—if at all.

as the weight is thrown to the right, is to raise the left side sharply. If this is done, it is bound to raise the arc of the swing. The ball will be hit on the upstroke and usually above its center.

A swing with this kind of body action almost invariably will be a quick lift of the club head going back and a chop coming down. If you doubt that you are chopping, here is a test you can make for yourself:

Go to a spot where the grass is 2 or 3 inches high. Now take some practice swings and watch to see whether the club head is brushing the grass for 6 inches before it reaches the ball. It should. If it isn't, then you are coming down too sharply from the top, which also will mean that you are lifting the club on the backswing rather than swinging it back, and you can work on that correction.

This "grass test" is one of the cheapest lessons in all golf, and you can give it to yourself.

You can make it a "dust test" too if the required grass is not handy. On bare ground the club head should raise dust a few inches behind the ball. If it doesn't, it means the same thing—that you are chopping. Don't fail to make use of these tests if you are topping.

As for straightening out the right knee on the backswing, this has precisely the same effect. It raises the body and with it the arc of the swing. It simply doesn't raise it nearly as much as stooping at the address and then rising.

The antidote here, of course, is not to straighten and lock the right knee. It should be slightly bent at the address and should remain slightly bent all through the swing until the ball is hit.

This is an insidious fault, however, against which a player inclined to top must be constantly on guard.

If cures for all of these reasons for topping fail, if you find after you have eliminated jerking the head up, swaying, and raising the arc, that you still top the ball, there are two things left to do. One is to have your pro check the loft on your wooden clubs. They may have less loft than they should have. He can remedy that. If that doesn't work, then our best advice is to consult an oculist. It is quite possible your eyes need a thorough examination.

SUMMARY OF CORRECTIONS
FOR TOPPING

Check jerking the head up.

Check swaying either to right or left.

Check raising arc of swing. Don't stoop but stand as erect as possible. Be sure right knee doesn't straighten and lock on the backswing. Don't dip left side or keep weight on left leg in backswing.

CHAPTER SIX

SMOTHERING

THIS CHOICE little number can kill all your better instincts unless you correct it quickly. It is a deadening, soul-searing thing that can descend on you suddenly and blight your afternoon completely. Like so many faults it usually manifests itself with wooden clubs, particularly tee shots. This leaves the smotherer struggling to recover from the rough on each hole and the harder he struggles the worse he usually becomes.

We once played with a chap who scored in the low 80's normally. This particular day he was in a spell of smothering—right from the first tee. There were 14 wooden-club tee shots on that course, and my friend smothered exactly 14 of them. To make matters worse there was more trouble on the left side of the fairway than on the right, and since most smothered shots go to the left my friend was knee deep in rough, with his back to a fence or a tree most of the afternoon. He finished with a 98 and almost gave up the game for life.

HOODED CLUB FACE

A smother is caused, of course, by a club face that is hooded at the moment it strikes the ball. The loft that the manufacturer built into the club face not only is eliminated

Fig. 32. Hitting with a club face turned over like this will never get the ball off the ground. This face is "hooded," and the picture shows a perfect contact for a smothered shot.

but actually reversed by the turning over of the club head. It is impossible, therefore, to hit the ball into the air. It must go into the ground quickly.

There are several degrees of smothering, depending on how much the club head is turned over. If its loft is altered slightly you may get a very low ball that will carry, perhaps, 100 yards. More of an alteration will drive the ball into the rough in front of the tee only 20 or 30 yards. But if the club face is completely hooded, the ball will strike the turf before it even leaves the teeing ground only 2 or 3 feet from the wooden peg. When it does this it usually will take a big hop and disappear in the rough short of the fairway. You will be able to see the impression where the ball hit in the turf of the tee.

When you reach this condition, brother, it's time to get help and get it in a hurry.

So, since a hooded club face is the reason for smothering, what is the reason for a hooded face?

There are two reasons: (1) A poor grip and (2) a bad position at the top even with a correct grip.

Either one of these will cause the right hand to overpower the left hand on the downswing, thereby turning the club head over until the face is hooded.

The Grip

Let's take the grip first. If the left hand or the right hand, or both, are placed too far to the right on the shaft at the address, the club face will be closed at the top of the swing. If it is closed at the top, it will be closed at impact. If the face is thus closed to the point where it is actually hooded, you will get a smothered shot.

Whether you get a smother or a hook depends on the degree to which the face is closed. If it is closed only slightly you will get a hook, but that is the best you may expect.

There is a simple, natural reason why placing the hands too far to the right on the shaft causes the club head to turn over. It is that by placing the hands this way, the wrists, especially the left, are put in a strained position. As soon as the left wrist begins to move at all, as in swinging the club back, it will revert immediately to its natural position, and as it reverts it turns the club head over. This reversion takes place on the backswing, which is why the face is closed at the top.

When you place your hands on the club be certain that not more than the knuckles of three fingers show. If you can see the fourth knuckle, your left hand is too much on top of the shaft. Move it back so you can see only three finger knuckles.

Now be sure that the V formed by the thumb and forefinger of the right hand points to your right shoulder—no farther. With this grip you will find the wrists in a natural, comfortable position. They won't turn on the backswing and close the face of the club.

So much for the grip. Now to correct the bad position at the top.

Position at Top

The position at the top that will cause a smother is mainly the position of the wrists.

Given the correct grip, the right wrist, not the left, must be under the shaft at the top. This will give you the half-closed club face at the top that is so necessary.

Fig. 33.   *Here we see one of golf's worst faults—a loose left hand at the top. The left wrist is under the shaft, the left hand bent back and opened. When this fellow starts his downswing, the first thing he will do is shut that left hand forcibly, which starts a "throw" of the club head and causes hitting from the top. Keep that left hand closed at all times. Don't take such a long, fast backswing that it will pull this hand open.*

If the left wrist is under the shaft at the top, the weaker left hand is bent backward and the fingers are loosened. Hence, when the downswing begins, the stronger right hand promptly overpowers the weaker left, made still weaker by being bent backward. And as soon as the right overpowers the left it closes the club face. If it is closed to the point of being hooded, the result is a smother.

However, if the right wrist is under the shaft, the right hand is weakened and the left strengthened. This keeps the left in command and hence prevents the club head from being turned over by the more powerful right.

If you are bothered by smothering, have someone watch nothing but your left hand at the top of the backswing. Quite possibly he will see this left hand open with the end of the shaft leaving the palm and being held loosely only by the fingers. This is a very bad position. It means the left hand has lost command and control and that the right hand will take charge on the downswing. Usually this position results from having the left wrist instead of the right underneath the shaft at the top. If the right wrist is under, the left hand won't tend to open at the top.

At times, of course, a bad grip and a bad wrist position at the top will be combined. Such teamwork will produce, as you can easily see, a bumper crop of smothered shots.

There are other things that will cause or tend to cause a smother. One of these is having the weight on the right leg instead of the left at the moment of impact. This means a collapsed left side, including the left arm. Another is pulling the head and shoulders up on the downswing. Both, however, take place in a swing that is radically wrong from the start. Neither occurs in a swing that is reasonably good. They are definitely minor reasons.

The major reasons are the grip and the position at the top.

SUMMARY OF CORRECTIONS
FOR SMOTHERING

Check grip. Be sure no more than knuckles of three fingers of left hand show at address. Be sure prescribed palm-and-finger grip is used with left hand. Be certain right-hand V doesn't point outside right shoulder.

Check position of wrists at top. Be sure *right* wrist, not left, is under the shaft.

Check club face at top. Should be half closed, never completely closed.

Check fingers of left hand at top. Make certain they grip club firmly. Must not be loose.

Check shoulder turn on backswing. Shoulders must turn on an almost horizontal plane. Left shoulder may be dipping on backswing, which can cause bad weight transference and a collapsed left side at impact.

Check shoulders on first movement of downswing. Must still be turned slightly to right of ball.

CHAPTER SEVEN

PULLING

A PULLED SHOT is one that goes in a straight line to the left of the target. It is the exact reverse of the push. Like the push, however, the pull may be combined with other bad shots, especially the slice.

In fact, the pull and the slice are of the same family, just as are the push and the hook. The pull is caused by an outside-in swing just as the slice is. But, where the slice is produced by an outside-in swing with the face open, the pull is the result of an outside-in swing with the face slightly closed (see Fig. 23).

In other words, the face is closed so far as the direction line is concerned but it is square to the line the club head is following—outside in. With this, obviously, you will get a straight ball to the left, the pull we have been talking about.

If the club face is closed not only to the intended line of flight but also to the direction the club head is following, you will get a pulled hook. The hook is dealt with in another chapter.

OUTSIDE-IN SWING

One thing is absolutely certain. A pulled shot is evidence of an outside-in swing, which is the worst swing you can have. If the worst you get from it is a pull, you are lucky. You are liable to get almost anything but a good shot.

So, in setting out to correct a pull, we must correct the outside-in swing.

What causes an outside-in swing?

There are two things: (1) A bad position at the top or (2) a wrong first movement on the downswing. And of course it is possible to combine these.

At the Top

To reach the correct position at the top we recommend strongly a careful study of the chapter on The Swing. In it we learn how to get to the top properly and what the right position there should be—must be—if we are to swing from the inside out.

The most important single movement in getting to the top correctly is the first movement of the backswing. This is starting the backswing *all in one piece*, dominated by the left side around a fixed axis. Such a movement, with body, shoulders, arms, hands, and club all moving together as though the player had no joints in his shoulders, wrists, or fingers, is absolutely necessary. It insures, above all else, that the club head will start back on the inside after the first 12 inches, that is to say, inside the projected line of flight. If it starts back outside this line, it will be virtually impossible to have it reach the top of the swing in a correct position. If it starts back outside, it will stay outside and when it comes back to the ball it will come from the outside in.

So start the backswing *all in one piece.*

Now as to the position at the top. To be certain of the correct position, all 12 points listed in the chapter on The Swing should be observed. The most important to insure hitting from the inside out are these:

Much more weight must be on right foot than on left.

The head must be fixed. No swaying.

Shoulders must be turned 90 degrees—a full pivot.

The *right* wrist must be under the shaft.

Shaft must point *across line of flight.*

Let's go over these in a little more detail If most of the weight is on the left foot at the top, it will shift automatically to the right foot at the beginning of the downswing. It has no other place to go. When this happens the right hip, and with it the hands, are thrown toward the front and right. This, in turn, throws the club outside the correct path and an outside-in swing is the result.

If we sway, which means we have not kept the head fixed, we move the whole axis of the swing to the right on the backswing. When we do that most of us leave it somewhat to the right on the downswing. If we take it to the right and leave it there, the chances are that we won't take a full pivot, that we won't have the club pointing across the line at the top, and that the club head will have passed the outside point of its arc by the time it reaches the ball.

This last point is sometimes overlooked. The club head should meet the ball at the extreme outside point of its arc as it swings down in front of the body. It reaches this point after coming from the inside, and after it reaches this point it begins, after traveling along the line of flight for a short distance, to come in again. But if the whole axis of the swing (meaning the body) has been moved to the right from its position at address, the outside point of the arc will have been reached *before* impact. Hence, the chances are that the club head will be moving back toward the inside at impact.

Don't sway. Keep the head and axis of the swing fixed.

A full pivot is equally necessary. If the shoulders are not turned a full 90 degrees, it will be virtually impossible to have the club pointing across the line of flight at the top. It's almost a physical impossibility. Also, with less than a full pivot, when the body turns back to the left sharply on the downswing, the shoulders are liable to turn much too far and by turning, throw the hands and club outside the line. Be sure the shoulders turn a full 90 degrees.

As to the third point—the right wrist being under the shaft—this is necessary to insure the command of the left hand. When the right wrist is under, the left hand retains its strength at the top, the naturally stronger right hand is weakened, and there is little tendency to throw the club from the top. When we hit from the top, the right hand is the one that does the hitting. By keeping the right wrist under the shaft at that point we weaken this hand so that it can't overpower the left and take charge. When it does take charge and throws the club from the top, it throws it outside the line and we hit from the outside in.

The fourth point is mandatory. Be certain the club is pointing *across* the line of flight at the top. Obviously, it will be easier from this position to hit from the inside out than if the club were parallel to the line or pointing away from it. If you will watch the backswing of the duffer or the average golfer, you will see that at the top his club almost always points *away* from the line of flight. You also will see that he swings from the outside in.

The expert, on the other hand, will have his shaft pointing *across* the line or at worst parallel to it and will be hitting from the inside out.

So why not do it the right way, the way the experts do it?

Coming Down

Apart from a bad position at the top, the only other thing that can cause an outside-in swing is a wrong first movement of the downswing.

The first movement coming down should be the return of the hips to their position at address—*with no swinging motion of the arms or hands*. To put it another way, the hips go back to their address position and pull the rest of the body with them. This return of the hips pulls the arms and hands down from their high position at the top but without any help from the arms and hands. They come down in one piece retaining as much of the wrist cock as possible.

You will find that when the hips get back to their address position the left arm will have been pulled down until it is parallel to the ground with most of the wrist cock still preserved.

From this halfway-down position the hands and wrists go to work throwing the club head at the ball.

Fig. 34. This player is swinging down to the ball, and the artist shows him committing one of the most common faults—hitting from the top. With the hands at this point the club should not have come farther than the dotted outline. Instead, the player has thrown the club right from the top, and almost all the wrist cock has been used up. Another very bad feature of this swing is that the player's weight is still on his right leg. It should have shifted immediately to the left leg. This chap's hands and club are far ahead of his body turn, and he is certain to hit from the outside in. For a pulled shot at contact, see Fig. 23.

The big point is that once you reach the halfway-down position correctly it will be impossible then to hit from the outside in. You will have to hit from the inside.

If, however, the hands and arms start to swing the club from the top as the hips go back to the address position, they will throw the club outside the line and the stroke will be from the outside in.

The great tendency in golf is to swing the hands *as* the hips turn instead of waiting until *after* they've turned, which is why there are so many scores over 100.

SUMMARY OF CORRECTIONS
FOR PULLING

Check outside-in swing. If you pull consistently you must be swinging from the outside. Correct that first.

Check start of backswing. Must be all in one piece so club can start back inside.

Check position at top. Weight must be on right foot, there must be no swaying, shoulders must have turned full 90 degrees, right wrist must be under shaft, and shaft must point across line of flight.

Check first movement of downswing. Hips must lead, hands follow. Don't start them together.

Check shoulder turn on backswing. Shoulders must turn in an almost horizontal plane. No dipping of left shoulder.

Check grip at top. Must be no loosening of hands or fingers on club.

Check shoulders on first movement of downswing. Must still be turned slightly to right of ball.

CHAPTER EIGHT

PUSHING

A PUSHED SHOT is usually a straight ball that goes to the right of the target. We say usually it is a straight ball because at times it can develop into a slice as well as a push. When a shot starts out to the right and then begins curving to the right, well, you are just lucky if you ever find it. The next county is the best place to start looking.

Fortunately a pushed shot doesn't rank among the worst faults in golf. In fact, it is not too bad a shot because it must be delivered with an inside-out swing, and an inside-out swing is the correct swing. So there isn't so much that is wrong with a wallop that produces a push.

A pushed shot is caused by hitting with a slightly open face while the club head still is traveling from the inside out. This condition can be brought about by (1) the body being ahead of the ball, (2) a very flat swing, or (3) playing the ball too far back.

The consequence of any of these is that when the club head reaches the ball the face of the club is still slightly open. It is open to the intended direction line but square to the line the club head is following. Since it is square to the line the club head is following and the club is still traveling from the inside out, it produces a straight ball.

Only when the face is not square to the line the club is following is a curving shot produced.

Fig. 35. Here is the usual position at contact for a pushed shot. The body is ahead of the ball, the swing is sharply from the inside out, and the club face is open. Give particular attention to the club face. It is traveling along the dotted line (a), and it is square to this line. The correct direction line is (b), and to this line the face is open.

BODY AHEAD OF BALL

Now, in the first cause given, the face is open and the club head is traveling from the inside out at the moment of impact because the body is ahead of the ball. In other words, the axis of the swing, instead of being opposite the ball has been moved to the left of it. Therefore, the arc of the swing won't reach its extreme outside point until *after* the ball has been hit. It should reach this outside point at the moment of contact.

What, you may ask, is the reason for the body being ahead of the ball?

There are two answers: A sway to the left on the downswing past, or to the left of, the position at the address, or playing the ball too far back toward the right heel.

Sway to Left

The effect of the sway to the left is that it puts the body well ahead of the hands and club head at the moment of contact. The hands, therefore, are deprived of the opportunity to "work," to whip the club head through the ball. They don't have the chance to quite close the face of the club to a 90-degree angle to the intended direction line.

In this pushed shot the club face reaches its correct position—square to the direction line—a few inches beyond where the ball was. This is because the forward sway has moved the center of the swing beyond the ball. The effect is the same as if the body had not swayed but the ball had been placed several inches back from the correct position. There again, with an inside-out swing, the club face would reach the ball before the hands had a chance to bring it square to the direction line.

Now to get at the root of the trouble.

The sway to the left on the downswing can be caused by one or both of two things: (1) Jerking the head up and/or (2) a sway to the right on the backswing. Often these are combined.

Pulling the head up, of course, is a common fault. It means the head is not being kept fixed. The swing can be made all the way up and down until, near the end, the player can't wait to see where the ball goes and looks up.

If he just looked up and nothing more, it would be all right. But, unfortunately, when he looks up while swinging a club, he usually moves head and body at the same time. This movement to the left gets the body and hands ahead of the ball at the moment of impact.

Avoiding it is easy so long as the head is kept fixed. If you will keep your head in a fixed position until your right shoulder meets your chin and forces it up, you won't have much trouble—not from looking up, anyway.

The other thing that causes the sway to the left is a sway to the right on the backswing. Some golfers who sway to the right on the backswing compensate for it by swaying back to the left on the downswing—and they sway too far. In other words, they overcompensate and in so doing get their body and hands ahead of the ball.

So, it follows that the thing to be avoided at all costs is

the sway to the right on the backswing. The way to avoid it is to *keep the head fixed*. If it is fixed and doesn't move to the right on the backswing, then the body won't move and there will be no reason to compensate by returning it to the correct position. Getting it back to and stopping it at the right position on the downswing is infinitely harder than never letting it leave the right position in the first place.

A simple trick that will help you guard against swaying is this: If the sun is out, turn until you have it at your back and then take a practice swing, watching the shadow of your head as you do so. You can tell instantly if you are swaying either forward or backward. The use of a mirror indoors serves the same purpose.

Sometimes, of course, the double sway and jerking the head up are combined. When this happens the player may get a sliced push or just a very bad push.

However, if the causes are eliminated, the pushing will cease. And in looking for the causes, look first to the head. *Keep it fixed.* If it is it will stop both the sway and the looking up.

Flat Inside-out Swing

The second reason for pushing was a flat inside-out swing. This frequently is accompanied by a pronation of the wrists which results in opening the club face quickly on the backswing. Such a face will be open at the top. When this happens, the player usually will come down to the ball from the inside out but with a club face which is still open and the ball will fly out to the right. When such a player falls into a fit of pushing he often tries to get the club face around faster, with his hands. Then he will start hooking or smothering because the forced hand action will close the face or even hood it.

The remedy for all this is simple. It is merely to start the backswing *all in one piece*, as if the hands and wrists had no joints. Then the hands will not pull the club back sharply on the inside, the swing will not be too flat, it won't be exaggeratedly inside-out and there will be no pushed shot. Not hard, is it? Just remember to start back *all in one piece*.

Position of Ball at Address

The one other thing that can cause a pushed shot is the position of the ball at the address. If, instead of playing the ball about opposite the left heel, it is placed back nearer the right heel, it may well cause a push. For by moving the ball well back at the address, the body naturally is ahead of the ball at impact. The effect is the same as playing the ball from the correct position but swaying to the left on the downswing. In each instance the body gets ahead of the ball and the club head reaches the ball before the face can get square to the direction line. In each case the face, with an inside-out swing, is square to the direction the club head is following but still a little open to the intended direction line. There isn't enough time for the hands to get the face closed.

SUMMARY OF CORRECTIONS
FOR PUSHING

Check looking up. It may be a violent jerk-up and pull the body ahead of the ball and the clubhead.

Check swaying. A sway to the right on the backswing may be over-compensated by swaying too far to the left on the downswing. This, again, will get the body and hands too far ahead of the ball and clubhead.

Check a very flat swing. Hands may be starting back sharply to inside. Start back *all in one piece.*

Check position of ball. Play it opposite left heel. Don't get it back opposite right heel.

CHAPTER NINE

SKYING

HERE IS one of the peculiar and not too common bad shots of golf. It's the shot that soars high in the air and doesn't go very far. Skying is very disconcerting to the player who is afflicted with it but, usually, it isn't very serious because the trouble can be cleared up quickly.

We remember playing with a fellow one day who skied all his wooden-club tee shots. He put a tremendous amount of effort into each swing, hit the ball what seemed to be a resounding whack, but never had far to walk for his second shot. The ball just popped up high in the air and dropped to the fairway about 150 yards from the tee. To make matters worse for the one who was skying, the day happened to be a wet one and every time the club came down it smacked into the soggy turf, ripped up a hunk of it, and spattered copious quantities of mud.

A skied shot is the exact reverse of the topped one. In a topped shot contact is made with too much of the face of the club above the center of the ball. In a skied shot, contact is made with too much of the club face below the center of the ball.

LOW CONTACT WITH BALL

What causes this low contact and a skied ball?
A forward sway with a chop is the usual reason. In such

a swing the club and the body have been lifted abruptly on the backswing with almost all the weight shifted to the right leg. Then the weight, as well as the club, is brought down sharply. The body moves to the left and the hands are well ahead of the club. The club head comes down just slightly behind the ball and, since it is traveling downward at a sharp angle, it hits ground and ball at the same time but *only the top of the head hits the ball*. This is why white ball marks appear on the top of the club head when a player is in a streak of skying.

Strangely enough this same swing can produce a topped shot as well as a skied one. If the sway to the left is far enough, it will bring the club head down virtually on top of the ball, which never will get off the ground. And, with a chopping stroke, if the club face does happen to meet the ball squarely, a very low shot will result.

It is a fact that this chopping swing with a forward sway will produce popping, topping, and low-ball hitting. Which one depends on just how the club face makes contact with the ball—early, late, or somewhere in between.

A swing in which the club head travels parallel with the ground for several inches before making contact with the ball never will sky that ball. Remember that.

Hence, to stop skying we must strive for the correct swing that will bring the club head along the proper path—parallel with the ground, not descending sharply. To check yourself on this, use the grass test. See with a practice swing whether your club head brushes grass that is 2 or 3 inches long for 6 inches behind the ball. It should.

Fig. 36. The artist shows us here the contact for a skied shot, with the club face striking the ball below center. This player has lifted the club quickly on the backswing and then chopped down at the ball.

Chopping, like so many other faults, can be traced right back to the beginning of the backswing. If we lift the club quickly from behind the ball we certainly will be inclined to bring the club down just as sharply, or even more so.

Therefore, the first corrective step is to see that our weight is evenly divided between our feet as we address the ball. And then start the backswing *all in one piece*. If we do this our weight will shift naturally to the right foot. It will be there at the top of the backswing and it will flow back to our left as we bring the club down.

Starting the backswing *all in one piece* with the weight moving to the right foot will automatically eliminate any possibility of lifting the club. It will *swing* the club back and up. Once it is swung back and up, we never will bring it down like an axe. And if we don't do that, we won't sky the ball.

So you see again how important is the start of the swing. Once you are started right, you are on the path to a good shot, but from a bad start anything can happen.

TURNOVER OF CLUB HEAD

Another cause of skying is a pronounced turnover of the club head. This may or may not be combined with the forward sway and the chop. Often it is.

The turnover of the club head can come from one of two things. It can come from the right hand taking command on the downswing or it can come from the bad habit of rolling the wrists.

Fig. 37. *Now we see the position at the top which leads to a chop and a skied ball. Our erring friend has taken the club back with a quick lift, has kept too much weight on his left leg, and now is ready to come down on the ball as if he had an axe. He can either sky this shot or, hitting a little farther forward, top it.*

Strong Right Hand

So far as the first reason is concerned (the right hand taking command), the basic cause lies far back. It lies in a wrong position, usually of the hands and wrists, at the top of the backswing. We can hardly do more here than remind the reader to go back to the chapter on The Swing and study the correct position at the top.

If the hands are in such a position at the top that the left is weakened and the right strengthened, then the stronger right is sure to overpower the weaker left when the downswing starts. Correct your position at the top and see what happens.

Rolling of Wrists

If an exaggerated rolling of the wrists is causing the turnover, then the player simply will have to stop rolling. If he rolls his wrists the chances are he has read somewhere, probably in an old book on golf, that this rolling is necessary. Therefore he does it consciously, has made a habit of it. He must break that habit.

It is a fact that in some of the older books on the game this rolling of the wrists—pronation it is called—got a lot of attention. The persons who wrote those books weren't trying to give readers wrong advice. They actually believed it was necessary to consciously roll the wrists to the right on the backswing and then roll them to the left on the downswing.

Like several other points of form, this one was exploded by the modern slow-motion moving-picture camera.

You not only don't have to roll the wrists, but you positively should not permit it. When you do roll them, you open the face of the club too quickly as it goes back from the ball. At the top it is open to the fullest possible extent and from there, to get it closed again, you must roll the wrists to the left on the downswing.

The golf swing has been found by most people to be difficult enough without introducing into it some extra frills that make it harder. So keep those frills out.

Don't roll the wrists. Go back to the chapter on The Swing and find that the correct way to start the club back is *all in one piece* as though you had no joints in your hands, wrists, elbows, or shoulders. If you start it back *all in one piece*, you won't roll your wrists.

The relation of skying and rolling the wrists is that when you roll them to the right on the backswing, you must roll them to the left on the downswing—and you roll them too far.

When you do roll them too far, they turn the club head over. When it's turned over too far, you can't even hit the ball with the face of it. You hit the ball partly with the top of the club head.

And this, mates, is a perfect recipe for skying a golf shot.

You may have heard that the use of a high tee is also a cause of skying. It can be. But it is very rare. Most tees aren't built long enough for them to be an actual reason for hitting under the ball. Also, the average player won't sky a shot even from a high tee. But a chronic skier will pop them up from a low one.

If you are using an extremely high tee it might be well to bring it down to normal height. But if you habitually sky the ball, don't count on the lower tee to snap you out of it. The cause goes deeper than that.

SUMMARY OF CORRECTIONS FOR SKYING

Check your swing for a chop. Use the "grass test."

Check lifting the club quickly on backswing. Be sure you swing it back and up starting *all in one piece.*

Check sway to left. Head must remain fixed.

Check too much weight on left foot at address and impact. Weight should be evenly distributed at address.

Check turning over of club head at impact. Be sure you are not rolling wrists.

Check right wrist at top. Be sure it is under shaft. Use all guards against right-hand domination.

CHAPTER TEN

SCLAFFING

THIS IS not too common a fault. The expert is virtually never guilty of it and the 80 shooter rarely. Once the 90's are reached, however, hitting behind the ball begins to appear with some frequency. From there up it may be encountered often.

Basically, sclaffing comes from practically a complete violation of nearly all the rules of form. It starts with a pronounced bend of the left knee on the backswing. This, in turn, means a wrong transference of weight. The weight on the backswing has been put on the left foot instead of the right. With the bending of the left knee, the left shoulder and the head drop. The head, you see, hasn't maintained its fixed position. It should not move up or down any more than it should move laterally.

The weight on the left foot restricts the pivot sharply so that the club can't go back on an inside line.

So now we have a golfer who, at the top of his abbreviated backswing, has done so many things wrong that his grip and the position of his arms and wrists no longer matter much—even if they are correct.

When this fellow starts his downswing he does it right from the top. He starts it by throwing the club head which is the worst thing he could do. And since his weight is al-

Fig. 38. *If you want to hit the ground behind the ball, this is an excellent position to be in. This chap has so much weight on his left leg that his left heel hasn't even come off the ground. The next thing he'll do is straighten that left leg and throw his weight back to his right. Then when he chops down at the ball he'll do what you will see in Fig. 39.*

ready heavily on his left foot, he shifts it sharply to his right foot.

The combination of the weight going back away from the shot and the club being thrown from the top almost invariably causes the club head to hit the ground behind the ball. The bending of the left knee on the backswing also tends to make many players bend the right knee on the downswing. And this, coupled with the wrong weight transference and hitting from the top, makes certain that dirt will fly behind the ball.

In short, one cause of sclaffing is a complete reversal of the correct weight transference—from left foot to right on the downswing, instead of from right to left.

The cure here is pretty obvious. The first thing to do is to start the backswing *all in one piece* without dipping the left knee, and keep the head fixed. Let the weight flow to the right foot as the body turns to the right.

If this is done until the top of the backswing is reached, there will then be no tendency to bend the right knee or drop the head on the downswing.

Once the correct position at the top is reached (and for that we once again refer the reader to the chapter on The Swing), there will be little danger of hitting too soon.

What danger there is, however, can be entirely eliminated by making the first movement of the downswing a turn of the hips to the left. This hip turn, with no swinging action of the arms, wrists, or hands, will bring the hands and club part way down all in one piece. From that position hitting from the top or hitting too soon is impossible. Equally unlikely

*Fig. 39. Now we see what happens from the position in Fig. 38.
The weight has gone back to the player's right, and his chopping
swing has brought the club head into the ground instead of the ball.*

will be ducking, dropping the right side, or bending the right knee on the downswing.

All of which brings us, in the case of sclaffing, to a point made many times before in this book. This is, merely, that if the swing is begun correctly, the chances of a bad shot are greatly decreased. And, conversely, if it is begun badly, the chances for a good shot are few.

The fundamental of starting the backswing *all in one piece*, around the head as a fixed point, with the left side dominating, can't be emphasized too much. It is the basis of a good swing, and if it is followed it will eliminate a multitude of evils.

It is not enough, for instance, for a sclaffer to be told simply not to drop his right shoulder. If that is the only thing he is told, the advice is wasted and he continues to hit behind the ball. He ducks or drops his right side because his *whole swing* is wrong. If it were right he wouldn't duck for there is nothing in the correct swing that impels a golfer to duck. So if his swing is corrected, the ducking stops and so does hitting behind the ball.

There is one other swing that will produce a sclaff. This is the one the better players sometimes fall into when they are deliberately trying for something else.

You've probably seen this happen. A good player takes his stance. He has teed the ball opposite his left heel but as he waggles the club he bends the upper part of his body to the right, dropping his right shoulder in pronounced fashion. His body, instead of being approximately vertical, is curved like a bow, the right shoulder very low, and more weight on the right foot than on the left. This player is trying to be certain he hits that ball squarely in the back in order to get the maximum distance, but his position is an open invitation to sclaff.

With his right shoulder low, his body bent to the right, and an unhealthy load of weight on the right foot at address, what happens? That's right. He comes down behind the ball, but not always, by any means. He may have been playing his shots that way for a long time and with good results because he has compensated by a lateral shift to the left on the downswing. This brings the club head to the ball instead of into the ground at the bottom of its arc.

Still, the invitation to sclaff always is there and, despite the fact this fellow probably hits a very long ball, he'll also sclaff one once in a while.

Why, though, should you or any average player invite a fault? There is no reason for you to drop your right shoulder and throw your weight on your right foot at the address. If you do, you simply set up a fault that you must find some way to overcome. As we have said before, compensations are for the expert. Why do it the hard way?

SUMMARY OF CORRECTIONS
FOR SCLAFFING

Check transference of weight. Must go from left foot to right on backswing and from right to left on downswing. Reversal of this order brings sclaffing.

Check dipping of left knee on backswing. Must not dip.

Check dropping of right shoulder, either at address or on downswing.

Check beginning of backswing. See that it starts *all in one piece* and that head does not drop. Head must remain fixed.

Check hitting from top. Don't throw club from top of backswing. Be sure first motion is hip turn to left.

CHAPTER ELEVEN

SHANKING

HERE, FRIENDS, is what is generally regarded as the most mysterious shot in golf. And, since psychologists tell us that it is the unknown that terrifies, shanking also is the most terrifying shot in golf.

When you recall what happens to a shanked ball, that it flies off to the right almost at right angles to the intended direction, and doesn't go far at that, you realize why it is so feared.

Another reason the shank is so dreaded is that it strikes without warning. Often a player is enjoying a pretty good round. He has been playing well, is having a tight match, comes up to a 150-yard approach to a green—and shanks. Immediately this player's confidence is utterly destroyed. The thought of a shank never had entered his head, perhaps, up to that point. But from then on he will fear it every time he takes a club in his hand. Fearing it and hence trying to steer the ball, he will be very lucky indeed if he doesn't shank again before the round is over.

This fear of a shank is not confined to dubs or amateurs. The pros dread it just as much, although they aren't guilty of it so often. Another thing about the shank is that it is contagious. To even see a player shank is sometimes enough to send the watcher into a fit of the same malady. In fact, there are some pros, even, who won't give a lesson to a shanker, because if they do they will have to stand and watch him shank. This, they fear, might send them into a spell of their own.

There was, for instance, a national open champion who was approached by a club member one day for a lesson.

"O.K.," said the pro, "I've got about 20 minutes right now. Get your clubs and we'll go to the practice tee."

The member got his clubs and started walking to the tee with the pro.

"What seems to be the matter?" asked the champion. "What are you doing?"

"I'm shanking," came the answer.

The pro stopped in his tracks.

"Oh, no," he said. "I won't be able to handle you. My assistant will take care of you."

From this instance you will get the general idea that nobody, even a national open champion, wants any part of a shanker. This is regrettable too, because no one needs help more or quicker.

The fact that there is so much difference of opinion as to what a shank actually is, is one of the reasons it is so feared.

A shank occurs when the ball is struck with the shank of the head instead of with the club face. That is how it gets its name. The face of the club never touches the ball. Contact is made a half inch or more off the heel of the club where it curves upward sharply. After a shot of this type, the white mark of the ball can be seen clearly on the inside of the club's shank. It glances off the club-head side of the shank which causes it to go sharply to the right.

What possibly could cause anyone to hit a ball in this strange manner?

The answer is a highly exaggerated outside-in swing, coupled with very little pivot and very loose, quick wrist action.

The swing that produces a shank is so much on the outside that at the moment of contact the entire club face is outside the ball. The only part of the club, then, that possibly can hit the ball is the shank.

It might well be said that, if a straight ball is obtained by a swing that is correct in every detail, a shank occurs with a swing that is wrong in every detail. There will, for instance, be a restricted pivot, little shoulder turn, loose wrists, usually a wrong distribution of weight, a pronounced throw from the top, and the swing will be from the outside in. There aren't many more things that can be wrong (see Fig. 21).

There are two swings, particularly, which tend to produce a shank. In one the player starts back more or less to the inside but with a quick break of the wrists. Then, with a restricted pivot, he throws the club from the top to the outside. The club head actually describes a big loop on this swing from the inside to the outside and makes contact with the ball on the shank. The other swing that will cause a shank is the one that starts back from the ball on the outside and is accompanied by a quick throw from the top. This is even worse than the first one, but both are very bad. Not only must there be no quick break of the wrists on the backswing, but the wrist cock must be retained coming down as

Fig. 40. The artist drew this merely to show you what a shank actually is. You will notice that contact with the ball is not being made with the face of the club at all, but with the shank of the club head. The face looks slightly open, and it usually is with a shanked shot. For a position at the top which can lead to shanking, see Fig. 21.

long as possible. Get the idea of bringing the arms, hands, and club down from the top *all in one piece*, a similar action to starting the backswing the same way.

Therefore, in correcting a shank, we must start from the very beginning of the backswing and make the various movements correctly instead of incorrectly.

This means, of course, starting the backswing *all in one piece*, letting the weight flow from the left foot to the right, keeping the left arm straight, turning the shoulders a full 90 degrees, keeping the right wrist under the shaft, having the shaft at the top point across the line of flight and restricting the wrist action.

The shank occurs when these things are not done. They are not done by a person who plays good golf only because of overanxiety. He permits his anxiety to hit a straight ball—steer the ball—to destroy his form. In that respect the cause of shanking is very largely mental. If instead of trying so hard to steer the ball he would try equally hard to perform the mechanics of the swing correctly, regardless of where the ball went, he would get his straight ball.

What often happens is this: A golfer starts his round with a pretty good swing. He hits the ball well and scores well. Along about the 12th or 14th hole the match is tight. He tries harder. He knows he must keep hitting the ball straight, so he begins to steer it. When he does this he shortens his backswing and restricts his pivot without realizing it. This causes him to hit from the outside a little. Then he begins to pull the ball. He tries harder to steer it. He pulls it even more, and before he knows what has happened he makes a supreme effort to keep it straight—and shanks it. The swing has gotten so much on the outside, his pivot is so restricted, and his wrist action so quick and loose, that he is lucky to hit the ball at all.

It has been our observation that almost invariably a player will be pulling the ball before he shanks it. We have seen it happen, and we have been told it by many of those who have come to us for help. We have asked those who have come for lessons what they were doing before they started to shank, and almost invariably they have told us, "pulling." We have checked this by looking at the faces of their clubs. The ball marks appeared on the heel rather than on the center. A pulled ball usually is hit on the heel and, furthermore, a pulled ball is proof positive that the swing has been from the outside in.

The answer to shanking, then, is to start virtually at the beginning and rebuild the swing—a swing that has collapsed under pressure.

If the player who is suffering is a reasonably good player, playing around in the 80's or 90's, this will not be hard. He will have to regain the feel of the correct swing and then use it often enough to make it a habit.

And he must remember, above all, to make that correct swing, to concentrate on making it when the pressure is heaviest. He must convince himself that the best way to hit a straight ball is to swing correctly, not try to steer it.

There is one other type of player who gets into the shanking habit. This is the chap who thinks he is a cut-shot artist. He tries to cut all his pitch shots or other short ones, opening the face of the club at address and deliberately hitting with an outside-in swing in an attempt to "cut the legs" from under the ball and give it terrific backspin.

Hitting cut shots is a job for the expert, not the dub. When the latter tries it he takes the first step toward shanking—and it's a big step. If he keeps trying to cut those pitches he will, without realizing it, open the face of the club more and more and swing farther and farther from the outside until. . . . Well, you know the answer. He'll come down with a case of shanking that may take months to cure.

So leave the cut shots for the Nelsons, the Sneads, and the Hogans. Don't open or close your face at address, and swing from the inside out.

SUMMARY OF CORRECTIONS
FOR SHANKING

Go back to first principles and check everything from correct grip to correct position at top and correct first movement of downswing. They probably all are out of kilter.

Work on all points that produce an inside-out swing, such as starting back *all in one piece*, having the weight well distributed at the top, firming up the wrists and starting down *all in one piece*.

Be sure the first movement of the downswing is with the hips, not the hands.

Concentrate on swinging correctly, not on where the ball goes

PART THREE

CHAPTER TWELVE

IRON PLAY

ALL THAT has been written in this book up to this point has dealt with corrections of bad shots and with the correct grip, stance, and swing. Generally speaking, these corrections hold true for all the wooden clubs and for the irons from the No. 1 to the No. 4. With these clubs the swing, for the average player, is always a full one and therefore it corresponds to the swing taken with the driver.

Of course, there are some (but very few) details that are different. When the irons are being used the player is forced to stand somewhat closer to the ball. The only reason for this is that the iron clubs are not as long as the woods. So, if we did not stand closer to the ball with the irons, we would have to bend over to reach it. And bending over is just as great a fault with the irons as with the woods. Stand as erect as possible for all shots.

Another slight difference is that with the long and medium irons the ball is played virtually midway between the feet instead of opposite the left heel. Playing the ball midway between the feet enables the club head to strike it a descending blow. A descending blow helps the natural loft of the club to impart backspin to the ball, which in turn helps to stop it quickly after it lands. With the wooden clubs we don't want to stop it quickly and therefore have no need to hit a descending blow.

Virtually everything else, however, is exactly the same with the irons as with the woods. Such things, for instance, as the grip, starting the backswing *all in one piece*, keeping the head fixed, the left arm straight, the right wrist under the shaft, the face half closed at the top, and the shaft pointing across the line of flight at the top. Also the same is the first movement of the downswing, which is the return of the hips to their position at address, drawing down the club, hands and arms all in one piece before the hands start to work. Likewise, swaying, dipping, or rising will spoil an iron shot just as quickly and completely as they will a full drive.

Iron shots can be hooked, sliced, pushed, pulled, topped, sclaffed, or shanked just as well as a full drive and for exactly the same reasons. They also can be smothered, although because of the greater loft of iron clubs, the effect is not as great as when a wood shot is smothered. Iron shots likewise can be skied but for a different reason than wooden-club shots. They can be skied by hitting them with a slightly open face and not with a descending blow.

If the ball is picked off the turf cleanly, without any divot and with a slightly open face, the ball will fly high. It will fly higher and not so far as when it is struck correctly. However, if the swing is correct, with the ball played midway between the feet instead of to the left, it will be struck a descending blow and won't be picked off cleanly.

So, if you are having trouble with iron shots, down to the No. 4 anyway, look for the cause and the correction in any of the chapters that fit your case. There are no more bad shots with the irons, and no fewer, than there are with the wooden clubs.

SHORT PITCHES AND CHIPS

From the No. 5 to the No. 9 the swing changes in only two respects. It becomes shorter, and at the top the weight is more evenly distributed between the feet than in the full swing. We don't mean by the latter that there should be more weight on the left than on the right, at the top. We mean merely that there should be a little less weight on the right than normally—a more even distribution.

The swing with the pitching clubs naturally becomes more upright because the clubs themselves are shorter and the player must stand closer to the ball. Also, the club is not taken back far enough for it actually to point across the line of flight at the top. However, the swing must still be made from the inside out, and to produce such a swing all the fundamentals must be observed.

If you are running into trouble with short pitches, the chances are that you are using entirely too much wrist action. This not only is a cardinal fault but by far the most common. The average golfer almost invariably uses too much wrist action on short pitch shots. Women are even more susceptible than men, and even many professionals with pretty high ranking are too "wristy" with their short pitches and chips.

Apparently there is a natural and overwhelming tendency on short pitch shots, and particularly chip shots, to bend or "break" the wrists as soon as the club head leaves the ball on the backswing. The reason this tendency is so strong may be because the shot is short and of the precision variety and the player feels it should be executed mostly with the fingers. So he tries to use hands and fingers alone. As soon as this takes place the wrists immediately are neglected and the hands swing the club like a pendulum from very loose wrists. The wrists stay in virtually the same position but "break" sharply on the backswing. And they break again, the other way, as soon as the ball is hit.

This is entirely wrong.

The wrists must be firm with as little break as possible. Try for no break at all and you will get about as much as you should get, for there must be some.

Just as in taking the club back on a full drive you strive not to break the wrists until the club forces them to bend, just so should you keep them from breaking quickly on the short pitches and chip shots.

A good professional, playing this short pitch or chip correctly, will take the club back a very short distance and with what seems to be no wrist action at all. Of course there is some. But not much. And it comes late—very late. You may have watched a pro make this shot and have thought, from the short length of his backswing, that the ball never would reach the green. Then you have been surprised that it actually went past the cup. You have been fooled because there was so little wrist action and what there was came so late.

Consistency and accuracy are the prime essentials in short pitches and particularly in chip shots. You never will get either one with loose, sloppy wrist action. Cut it down.

Fig. 41. *A most common cause of bad iron play is a quick wrist break on the backswing. This player has "broken" his wrists as soon as he started the club back. His weight hasn't even started to move to his right leg. When he gets to the top he'll uncock those wrists just as quickly as he "broke" them, and he'll hit from the top far too soon.*

Quite a few players run into trouble by topping short pitches. Few things are so disconcerting. You are trying to drop the ball close to the pin and, instead, you half top it and see it bounce into a trap or skitter over the green.

In addition to the usual reasons for topping, pitches are sometimes topped through failure to keep the left arm straight on the downswing. This is caused by the temptation to guide or steer the shot with the right hand because it is a delicate shot. This, in turn, causes us to forget the left. If we forget it, it may collapse slightly. As soon as that happens the radius of the swing is destroyed. It becomes shorter and hence the club head fails to quite reach the ball. This is all that is necessary to cause a half top.

Keep that left arm straight, right down and through the ball.

In chip shots, of course, the backswing is so short that the wrist action should be negligible. The chip that rolls up and nestles close to the cup is the greatest stroke saver in the game, but you cannot make that shot consistently with loose wrists. They must be firm in chipping, beyond all other shots.

When the wrists are firm they move backward and forward in making the shot, so that the club face opens very little on the backswing and doesn't close at all after the ball is hit. It is extremely important to keep the face *still at right angles to the direction line after the ball has been hit.* This can be done only with firm wrists. With loose wrists the face will open wide on the backswing and close as soon as the ball is hit. Consistent accuracy is almost impossible with a swing like that.

Fig. 42.   Here we see the late wrist break, with the backswing being started all in one piece and the weight shifting naturally to the player's right leg. This restricted wrist action is especially important with irons.

Fig. 43. Above is the correct finish of a chip shot, in which re-stricted wrist action is most important. Notice how firm the wrists are and, particularly, that the face of the club is still square to the direction line. The firm wrists never have permitted it to close. This chip will be right on the line.

Fig. 44.   Here is the wrong finish of a chip shot. This one has been
made with loose wrists, wrists which have not gone through with the
shot and have permitted the club face to turn over and close. This
man will be lucky if his chip isn't pulled badly to the left of the cup.

If your wrists are firm you will find that you hit the ball the same way all the time. You will not hit it halfway to the cup one time and 15 feet past the hole the next. You will not have it run like a rabbit on one shot and pull up sharply on another. With good, firm wrists your chip shots will behave dependably. And you also will find that they will be on the line more often than not. Sloppy wrists will produce a discouraging number of pulled or pushed chips, so that even if the range happens to be correct, the ball is too far to the right or left of the cup to make the putt an easy one.

Accurate chipping takes a great strain off the putting department.

For the short pitches the feet are closer together than for the long shots, and for chip shots they should be very close. In playing chips it is best to cultivate the habit of "sitting down" to the shot. Don't stoop over the ball but bend the knees slightly more than for the longer shots. Start to sit down—and then stop. You will quickly get the idea if you try it a few times.

Also it is best to shorten your grip on the club, open the stance somewhat, and have the hands just a little farther forward than for an ordinary iron shot.

Standing erect and gripping the end of the club simply will not give you the control you need for the delicate chip.

By having the hands slightly forward of the ball we do not mean to play the ball back off the right foot. If you do that, the chances are that you will stub the shot or top it. Either is disastrous. Simply play the ball between the feet, which are close together, and move the hands slightly forward.

A tendency to be avoided in chip shots is using the same club for all of them. Every golfer has a favorite club for this shot. It may be a No. 5 or No. 7. No matter which club it is, he will use it, regardless of whether the shot he has to make calls for it or not. He becomes so accustomed to using his pet club that he has no confidence in any others and simply won't use them.

Don't get into this habit; or if you have it, break it. It's a habit that is costing you strokes—and perhaps money. For instance, suppose your ball lies on the apron of the green, 2 feet from the putting surface, and suppose your favorite chipping club is a No. 7 or No. 8. Those clubs have a great deal of loft. You don't need loft for this shot. It is simply a long putt with only a little loft needed to make the ball reach the putting surface. From there it can roll toward the cup. You may well ruin the shot if you play it with a lofted club. All you need is a No. 4 or No. 5 iron that will supply the slight loft you need plus plenty of roll.

On the other hand, if your favorite chipper is a No. 5 and your ball is 20 or 25 feet from the putting surface, you will find it impossible to hit the required shot. The No. 5 won't give you the loft to reach the green and at the same time stop the ball anywhere near the hole. The ball will be well past the cup, if, indeed, it doesn't go right off the back of the green. This is the spot for the No. 7 or even, perhaps, a No. 9. With these you will get the loft necessary to reach the putting surface and the ball will drop with little run on it.

So school yourself to use a variety of irons for chip shots. Don't let your confidence in one club work against you.

Remember, always, that the chip is the great stroke saver. This is the shot with which the best players take up the "slack" when their long shots miss the mark. The ability to get down in two shots from the edge of the green is an invaluable asset. To take four from the edge is inexcusable.

So work on the chip shots. Use a variety of clubs. And, above all, restrict that wrist action.

CHAPTER THIRTEEN

PUTTING

HERE is the game within a game. Putting is half of the game of golf.

When you consider that par on any course includes two putts on every green, you see what we mean. On a par-72 course, for instance, 36 shots are allowed on the greens and 36 others to reach them. So, when we say that putting is half the game of golf, that's exactly what we mean.

Of course, for the average golfer who scores around 100 the shots he takes to reach the eighteen greens will outnumber the putts he takes. And for the expert, the player who is clinging close to par, or the top tournament player who is beating standard figures, 36 putts a round are decidedly too many. Even if the high-60's boys reached every green in the required number of shots, which they don't, they couldn't dig into the 60's with two putts per green. They have to do better than that.

In these days of red-hot scoring, 28 or 30 putts per round is considered to be about par for the top-flighters. Even twenty or twenty-five years ago you couldn't expect to win a big tournament with more than 32 putts a round. No matter how good you are, you're going to miss some of those greens when you shoot at them, and the only way that slack can be taken up is by one-putting.

The number of birdies scored these days is an indication

of the number of one-putt greens. Where once a player was satisfied to get down in three shots from 160 yards, your experts of today are gunning for birdies from farther away than that. They're planning to lay that approach shot close enough to the pin to hole out with their first putt.

The same is true of shots from traps around the greens. Today's topnotchers aren't satisfied merely to get out of the sand. They are figuring on getting out close to the cup. Of course, the improved sand irons, specifically the wedge, are partly responsible.

But on top of everything—greater accuracy with the irons, improved trap play, and a greater one-putt consciousness— is the undeniable fact of better putting. There may not be greater individual putters today than some of the old-time masters on the greens, but on the average they are better. The first 20 in a national open championship today will average fewer putts per round than the first 20 averaged 30 years ago.

What has caused this sharper putting? Endless experimentation, for one thing. The pros and top amateurs who ply the tournament circuit, winter and summer, spring and fall, are keenly aware of the value of putting, and they are trying constantly to improve the stroke.

Exactly what are they trying to do, you may ask? They are trying to find some method of stroking so that the face of the putter when it meets the ball always will be at precisely right angles to the direction line they have chosen. That's the dream and they are striving to make it come true.

Obviously, when a golf club is swung on any shot, the face

of the club opens and closes. It opens, or turns away from the ball, on the backswing. On the downswing it comes back to a position at right angles to the direction line and then closes, or turns away from the ball in the opposite direction.

The object on all shots is to have the face at right angles to the direction line at the moment it meets the ball. That's what governs the direction the ball takes.

Having the face at right angles at the moment of contact in putting is vitally important because a variation of a single degree is enough to cause the ball to miss the cup.

Now, with the face opening and closing, it reaches the 90-degree angle for only an instant. And in this instant the ball must be hit.

To cut down the chance for error in this most delicate stroke, the top putters of today are trying to keep the face from opening and closing as much as possible. They try to keep it square to the direction line at all times.

It is easier to keep the face from opening with a very short backswing than with a long one. And because of the construction of the human hand and wrist it is quite possible to keep the face from closing at all after the ball is struck.

This is exactly what the pros are doing now. Jug McSpaden is generally conceded to be the best putter today, and he uses a very short backswing, almost no wrist action, and his forward swing with the putter is almost a push, the face of the putter remaining at right angles as it follows out after the ball.

Such a putting stroke may seem to violate, we know, many of the rules for good putting that have been laid down for the last 25 years. We have all heard and read, no doubt, that a full backswing is essential in order to avoid jabbing the putt. That, we believe, has been disproved.

The stroke we have described, with the short backswing, almost an absence of wrist action, and a push through the ball, is not jerky. It isn't a jab. It is as smooth as satin once the rhythm of it has been established.

The keeping of the face at right angles to the line after the ball has been hit serves one great purpose. When it is done, it practically prevents pulling the ball to the left of the hole. And pulled putts—putts that miss on the left side of the cup—are the most common misses in all golf. With the chance for this one miss greatly reduced, there remain only two other places a ball can be sent—to the right of the cup or in it. With one less place for the ball to go, the number of putts you will hole will amaze you.

Now that you have the theory, let's see how the stroke is made.

THE GRIP

As with all other shots, we start the putt with the grip. That is the most important. And here again we violate the older tenets of good putting. We have been told that the palms should exactly oppose each other in a good putting grip. This may be all right for people gifted with the touch of a billiardist, but most of us don't have that. So we will offer the modern grip that attempts to substitute mechanics for "touch."

Instead of placing the left hand on the club with the palm facing directly away from the hole, place it so the palm faces directly out in front of you. Now place the shaft diagonally across the palm of the left hand and grip it with the last three fingers.

You will find that in closing the left hand the palm turns slightly away from the hole, but that when the hand is closed the palm is not turned away at right angles. It is still facing somewhat toward the front.

Now place the right hand on the shaft so that it, too, faces somewhat toward the front rather than toward the hole. The right hand takes a finger grip with all four fingers, and the forefinger of the left hand overlaps the fingers of the right. This forefinger will run diagonally down across the backs of two fingers of the right hand and perhaps three, depending on the length of your fingers.

With the left hand turned outward, the inside of the left thumb will rest against the shaft. The right thumb may be placed straight down the shaft or slightly across it. In fact, some players bend the right thumb sharply and dig the nail into the leather grip. You also may find that the tips of the last three fingers of the right hand will rest against the left thumb when the grip is complete, rather than against the shaft of the club. The position of the hands makes this almost inevitable.

Now what do we have? We have a grip in which both hands are under the shaft with the palms facing somewhat toward the front rather than toward each other and with the overlap reversed.

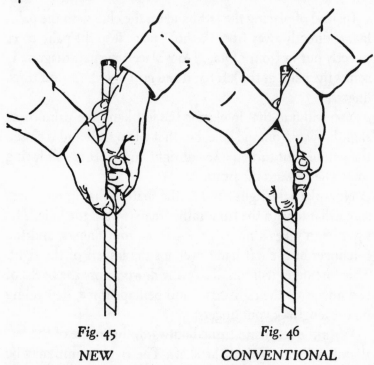

Fig. 45   Fig. 46
NEW   CONVENTIONAL

*Figs. 45 and 46. The new putting grip, with palms of both hands
facing slightly toward the front, is at the left. It doesn't look much
different from the conventional grip, but it feels a great deal different. In the conventional grip the palms are directly opposed. Notice
in the new grip how the forefinger of the left hand overlaps three
fingers of the right.*

Why do we have the palms of both hands "open," or facing away from us?

We have the left open because in this position it has
turned the left wrist slightly to the left. With the left wrist
turned thus, it is out of its natural position and its tendency

is to turn back toward the right. In any event it never will turn farther to the left. And since it won't, the face of the club will never close and the putt won't be pulled to the left of the cup.

By placing the right hand under the shaft, it, too, is out of its natural position. It will tend to turn to the left and this tendency, working against the left, virtually "locks" the left in position. The left won't turn farther to the left of its own volition and it can't turn to the right because the right hand is working against it.

The whole effect here is to keep the hands from turning either way and, therefore, to keep the face of the putter from turning either way. In short, the face will open but slightly and will never close with the putting motion. It will stay at right angles to the direction line as and after the ball is hit, which is exactly where we want it.

Another consequence of this grip with both hands under the shaft is that it tends to restrict the wrist action in the stroke and make the putt more of a hand and arm action. This we will describe immediately.

Thus are mechanics substituted for "touch" in putting, so far as substitution is possible. They won't make anyone a great putter overnight, but they will go far toward minimizing the mistakes that cause poor putting.

THE STROKE

Strange as it may seem for a shot as delicate as the putt, the stroke is made not with the fingers and wrists but primarily with the arms and hands. Fingers and wrists have their function, of course, but it is slight compared to that of the arms and hands.

The job of the fingers is simply to hold the club and not to move on the shaft. In other words, the grip must not be altered in the slightest.

The grip should not be too tight or too loose—merely firm enough to obtain the maximum of control. That's all.

As for the wrists, they bend or "break" only slightly; less, even, than for a chip shot. The wrist break for a putt can be felt by the putter but barely seen.

Only the arms and hands then, are left to make the stroke, and they make it. The backswing is a slight movement of the arms and hands to the right without bending the elbows. The forward swing is a movement to the left, through the ball, toward the hole.

In this movement the arms and hands swing from the shoulders. The bend in the elbows doesn't change by so much as a millimeter, nor is there a conscious bend of the wrists. The shoulder joint is the hinge of the putting "swing."

Never let the wrists "break" after the ball has been hit. Carry arms, wrists, hands, and putter out toward the hole with no bend whatsoever. ·

When this swing is made with the grip as described, the face of the putter will open very little on the short backswing, and it will not close on the forward swing more than it has opened. The head of the putter will be carried out toward the hole with the face still at right angles to the direction line.

Fig. 47. Here is the address for the putt. Most of the weight is on the left leg, the ball is played near the toe of the left foot, and the body is bent enough for the arms and hands to swing freely from the shoulders. The new grip also shows clearly.

149

Fig. 48. *Top of the backswing for a short putt. The big point to note here is that the face of the club has opened little if at all. This is most important.*

Fig. 49. Finish of the stroke for a short putt. Of vital importance here is that the hands and arms have swung through with the club, with almost no wrist action, and that the face of the putter is still square to the direction line. Never let it close.

With this stroke it is obvious that the chance for error has been reduced to a minimum. Since the face opens very little and closes not at all, there is no split second of time in which it must meet the ball while at right angles to the direction line. It is at right angles most of the time, and that is the whole secret.

The body, of course, must be kept still throughout the stroke—and the body includes the head. Don't let the shoulders or any part of the body turn toward the hole as the ball is struck.

The instant you turn your head or body toward the hole, you destroy the aim of the shot. Once that is gone, of what use is the proper grip, swing, or anything else? Keep the head anchored. Don't take a peek to see whether the ball is on the line. If it isn't, pecking won't put it there. And if it is on the line, you'll hear it drop. So don't look—*listen!*

The head of the putter always should be kept low and the backswing short, but aside from that there is nothing else to be done.

With a very short backswing you probably will get the feeling that you can't hit the ball as far as you want to. This feeling will vanish once you get the rhythm of the stroke. You will find that you can "push" the club head through— not at—the ball with almost any strength you desire, and the stroke will work just as well for long putts as for short ones. For the long ones the length of the backswing need not be increased much. You need only apply slightly more force to the forward swing of the arms.

You will have to practice to get the proper rhythm and

no one can explain in words what that rhythm feels like. You will know it when you get it.

We know that the grip and putting stroke we have described will feel strange to you. You probably will swear you never in the world will be able to use it. But don't give up on it. Practice it. Practice it again and again. Once you get the feel of it, once you find your ball dropping in the cup on those tantalizing 6-footers and resting close on the long ones, you'll like it.

What, you may ask, about the stance? Should it be open or closed? Should our feet be close together or wide apart? Where should our weight be? And should we stand erect or bend over?

Only the weight makes much difference. The weight should be more on the left foot than on the right, assuming the player is right-handed. In any event, more of it should be on the foot nearer the hole than on the other foot. The ball should be played somewhere near this near foot. The weight doesn't have to be 90 per cent on the near foot, but enough of it should be there to keep the body from swaying, enough to steady the body.

The other points don't matter much. Good putters like Bobby Jones have stood with their feet close together. Others have spread them wide. Walter Hagen, one of the greatest, used a wide spread for years and then brought his feet close. Many good putters have stood up straight. Others, equally good, have bent over. Most good putters use a slightly open stance. But a square or even a closed one still is all right.

Aside from the weight, your stance is your own. Any stance that permits a free swing of the arms and hands from the shoulder joints is stance enough.

GENERAL THOUGHTS ON PUTTING

Once the mechanics of the grip and stroke have been established, the only factor remaining for a good putt is good aim. This the player himself must acquire through practice and experience. Only experience and judgment will tell him how much he must "borrow" on a sloping green, how hard to hit the ball to make it reach the hole, or whether he should "borrow" at all on a short putt or instead hit straight at the cup.

Some players have found, or believed, that by pointing the left elbow toward the hole they have been able to aim the shot better. Perhaps they can. Maybe you can.

Others have believed that by a very slight firming of the grip of the last three fingers of the left hand just before the backswing is started, they steady the left and make it less likely to turn. Perhaps that is true. There are lots of little tricks like that in putting, and far be it from us to pass judgment on them. They might work for you and they might not.

So far as the selection of a putter is concerned, the tendency now is toward a heavy club. A heavy putter, it is felt, is less likely to get out of control than a light one. Also, a heavy one increases the feeling that the club is like a mechanical pendulum swinging from the shoulders. Perhaps, too, this move toward heavy putters stems from the feeling

good golfers have when they are "hot." They feel then that
their clubs are "heavy." When a player starts a round with
his clubs feeling "light," he is usually in for trouble. That's
the day his touch is lacking.

The putter definitely should have an upright lie. That is,
the angle between the shaft and the sole should be small
rather than large. A putter with an upright lie enables the
player to sole the club flat on the ground and still stand close
to and over the ball. A putter with a flat lie forces the golfer
to stand away from the ball. From this position good aim
is difficult.

Also the putter should have a slight loft. This raises the
ball slightly as it is struck and starts it straight along the
direction chosen. Bent-grass greens, such as we have on our
courses in this country, have a decided grain that affects the
direction of the ball when the grain runs to either right or
left. By using a putter with a slight loft, which raises the ball,
we at least can get it started straight.

Always study the grain before every putt. If it is at all
pronounced and if you have to putt across it, allow for de-
flection. If you are putting dead against the grain you will
have to hit the ball harder than you think or it will pull up
short of the hole. On the other hand, of course, a putt that
is with the grain all the way will run farther than you expect.

Also, when your ball is a long way from the hole and your
only object is to get it close so you won't three-putt, study
the grain around the cup. Find which way it runs. Then,
when you aim your long putt, make sure that when the ball
finally stops, your next putt won't have to be made *across*

the grain. You'll have a much better chance of sinking your second one if you can make it with the grain or even against it, but not across it.

You can follow the same plan with your chip shots. Whenever possible, hit them so you don't have a crossgrain to putt over.

Another point to watch is whether the green is dry, damp, or wet. This, usually, is obvious. Yet there are times when it isn't. These are when the night's dew hasn't completely evaporated and, again, late in the afternoon at certain times of the year when the dew falls early. Late in the afternoon, especially, you may not notice the dew. That's when you suddenly find yourself four or five feet short with no apparent reason. When that happens, feel the grass. It'll usually be damp.

Putting, as you see, is a game in itself. There are many players, probably one in your foursome, who are outstanding and appear to have been born great putters. Maybe they were. But the chances are they weren't. They became good only by practice—lots of it—and experience. That's the recipe.

CHAPTER FOURTEEN

OUT OF THE ROUGH AND TRAPS

SINCE THIS book is chiefly about trouble—and how to get out of it—it is only fitting that we should spend a little time in the tall grass and sand. No matter how good a golfer may be, he can't hit every shot perfectly. The best often stray from the straight and narrow path. So let's see what the procedure is when we find ourselves in the rough and in sand traps.

FROM THE TALL UNCUT

Play from both requires judgment, more judgment perhaps, than is necessary for a fairway or tee shot. The judgment consists of deciding how much to attempt from either the grass or the sand. There is always a great temptation, particularly from the rough, to try to get more distance than the lie of the ball indicates. When we get in the rough we know we have made a mistake. We are in trouble and our first thought is to get out of it with as little damage as possible.

And that, usually, is our second mistake. We take out a No. 2 iron and try to get distance where a No. 6 is called for. We hit the ball but we not only don't get distance, we don't even get out of the rough.

That is one of the worst mistakes a golfer makes. Untold

shots and headaches have been brought on by just that poor judgment. How much better it would be if, once in the rough, we would play out safely without thought of distance so that our next shot could be played from the fairway instead of again from the rough.

The first thought in a player's mind as he goes to find his ball in the rough should be this:

"I've made a mistake and I'm going to pay for it. Regardless of what lie I have in there, I'll play it out safely."

Once you have established that in your mind and carried it out, what is the picture? You have lost a shot. All right. You might have lost three or four more by trying to get distance from that rough.

But your ball is now in the fairway. If you can make up that lost shot, now is the time to do it. If you can make a good shot now, laying your ball close to the pin for one putt, you will escape the penalty of your first error—the shot that sent the ball into the rough.

You can do that only with a superlative shot. But—and here is the big point—you have a much better chance of making such a shot from the fairway than you ever could have from the rough. Isn't that reasonable? Isn't it hard enough to pull off a great shot from a good fairway lie than from the tall, tangled, or matted grass of the rough? Once out of the rough, however, you have that chance. But if your recovery fails, all hope is gone.

So play them safely from the rough. Don't plan for much, don't hope for much. Be satisfied to get out.

Now for the technique of playing from the uncut grass.

Generally speaking, the technique should be that of the pitch shot, a short, very upright swing, with a lofted club. The swing must be decidedly upright so the club head can hit the ball a sharply descending blow without getting too much grass at contact between face and ball.

The single most important factor is *loft*.

With a lofted club—a No. 5, 6, 7, 8, or 9, depending on the height of the grass—you will have a far better chance of getting out than you would have with a less lofted iron. And getting out is by far the most urgent job you have to do. Give it the No. 1 priority.

No set rule can be laid down as to just which club you should use from the rough. It is entirely a matter of judgment. You must decide that for yourself. But always remember to underclub. Never use from the rough the same club you would use from the fairway.

You will have the feeling, of course, that by underclubbing you will lose distance. You will. But to make your mind easier on this, you will not lose as much distance as you think you will and, what is even more vital, you will be out of the rough.

The reason you won't lose so much distance is because a shot from the rough runs when it hits the fairway. It runs because the tall grass gets between the face of the club and the ball. This forms a cushion of a sort and although it detracts from the force of the blow, it also prevents the club face from "gripping" the ball. Hence, no backspin is imparted and the ball falls "free" or even with a slight overspin when it lands. Therefore, some of the distance lost by playing a lofted club is regained by the run. So don't feel you are sacrificing too much distance by underclubbing. You're not. Besides, your ball will be out of the rough and on the fairway.

One extra word about playing from the rough. Don't put extra effort into the swing. Don't press. Concentrate on making the correct swing from the rough and not on getting the ball out through sheer power. It won't work.

Also, from a very bad lie, don't hesitate to use the sand wedge. Being heavy with a sharp sole, it will cut through virtually anything in the grass or weed department. It is a very useful tool from a nasty lie.

TRAP PLAY

Now for the dreaded traps.

Playing from sand, especially from bunkers around the green, is perhaps the most feared phase of golf. The knowledge that it is absolutely necessary to get the ball out of the sand, yet not hit it hard enough to knock it over the green, is terrifying to the duffer. Yet it shouldn't be, for the technique of playing from sand is no harder to learn and probably easier than playing from tee or fairway.

The best and safest shot from a trap is the explosion. This is true regardless of how the ball lies. If it lies in a heel print, you have no choice but to use the explosion. If it lies clean you can half blast it or, if the trap is very shallow, you even can chip it. But either of these shots is much more dangerous than the explosion. So explode. Forget the others.

The explosion consists, simply, of hitting an inch or an

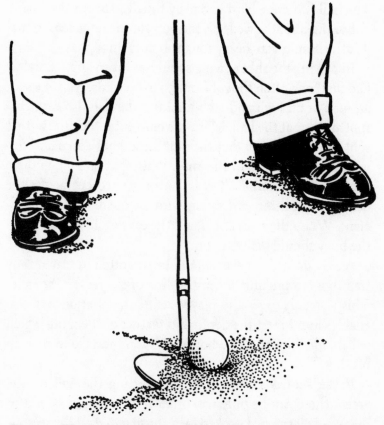

Fig. 50.   We don't like traps, and we want to get out of them. This is the way—by hitting the sand an inch and a half behind the ball. As the sand is thrown up, the ball will come with it. This shows the contact for an explosion shot, with the ball lying cleanly.

inch and a half behind the ball. The club head travels through the sand and comes up in front of where the ball had been. As it plows under it throws up plenty of sand and along with it the ball. The club face itself never touches the ball.

The ball is merely blasted out by the displacement of sand.

For this shot the wedge is the best for the same reason that it is the best in very heavy rough. It cuts through.

In playing the shot a swing should be taken approximately like that for a pitch shot of from 50 to 60 yards. Aim at a spot an inch or an inch and a half behind the ball. Look at that spot and not at the ball. Make the club enter the sand at that spot. And be certain that the club head goes *down and forward* and comes out of the sand. With that technique there should be no trouble. It is not necessary to cut across the ball. A straightforward swing with an open stance is sufficient. When the sand is wet, a little less should be taken and the blow should be less heavy.

An action which never should be forgotten in playing any trap shot is a preliminary embedding of the feet in the sand. This not only gives the player a firm foundation but also enables him to test the depth and texture of the sand, which will enable him to judge how much sand to take in making his shot.

If the shot is not successful in getting the ball on the green, there can be only two other results. It can be left in the trap or it can be knocked over the green. And the reasons for these are simple enough.

If the ball is still in the trap after the explosion, it is because too much sand was taken or because the shot wasn't carried through until the club head came out of the sand. Of course, it can also stay in the trap if it is topped, but if you are consciously trying to hit behind the ball you're not likely to top it.

If too much sand was taken the chances are that the swing was directed too far behind the ball. The remedy for that is simple and obvious.

If the club head didn't come out, it means merely that you have quit on the shot, that you didn't carry it through. You can't quit on a trap shot and get a good one any more than you can quit on any other shot.

Now, if the ball was knocked out of the trap and over the green, it means not enough sand was taken. Here again the cure is obvious. Perhaps you have been picking out a spot an inch behind the ball but have been looking at the ball. This won't do. This will tend to bring the club head against the ball rather than an inch behind it. *Look at the spot you pick out.*

Judgment in playing trap shots is the same, as we mentioned before, as in playing from the rough. The most common error is in trying for too much. Naturally when you are in a trap you are bound to think how fine it would be if you came out 6 inches from the cup, but that is just wishful thinking. You should be satisfied to get out somewhere on the green.

Suppose, for instance, on a par 4 hole that you have just put your second shot into a trap by the green. The ball lies well and you decide to try a half blast with the idea of getting within 3 or 4 feet of the cup. You can get down in one putt and get your par 4 anyway. You play it—and you miss. Your ball still is in the trap. Now you are lying three and you have absolutely no chance for a 4. The best you can get is a 5.

Wouldn't it be more sensible to play a full explosion on your third shot and get the ball somewhere on the green? Once on the green in three, you have a chance to get down in one putt for a 4, regardless of how far away you are. But if you have to play your fourth from a trap, all chance is gone.

So get the ball out.

CHAPTER FIFTEEN

UNEVEN LIES

PLAYING A ball from a lie that is anything but level is a problem of high magnitude for anyone but the expert. This is natural since the average golfer has problem enough in hitting a ball straight from a level lie.

But uneven lies can be handled if you know how. You can't, of course, hit the ball as straight from them as you can from a flat lie, but if you know the compensations that must be made, you at least can keep your ball away from the worst trouble.

Uneven lies fall into four categories—uphill, downhill, standing above the ball, and standing below the ball. That's not so many, and the means for handling them are not complicated either, so don't let these lies terrify you.

UPHILL LIE

Playing a ball from an uphill lie is perhaps the easiest of the four. The tendencies here are to take a big, full, hard swing, to hook or pull the shot to the left, and to underclub.

Resist the temptation of the big swing. Take a shorter grip, use a shorter backswing, and pivot less (because it is harder to keep your balance).

The reason you are inclined to hook or pull a shot from an uphill lie is that your weight is well back on your right foot and the body has a tendency to swing around to the left. Therefore, aim this shot a little to the right. If you are playing to a green, aim for the right-hand corner of it or at a trap on the right. Usually you will find the ball traveling toward the flag instead of the trap. And don't hit too hard.

As for the underclubbing, that takes place because the slope of the ground increases the loft of the club. If you hit the ball right from an uphill lie, you will get a higher and shorter ball than you would from a level lie. Hence, the easy solution is to use an iron (if you are playing an iron) one number lower than you would use for the same shot from a level lie, that is, an iron one number stronger. Then you will get the distance you expect.

DOWNHILL LIE

The downhill lie offers more difficulties. The tendency here is not to get the ball up and to slice or push it off to the right.

Most important in getting the ball up are the use of a more lofted club than you ordinarily would use and *staying down to the shot all the way through the swing.* The moment you raise the head, shoulders, or body on a downhill lie, you set in motion the movements for a topped shot. So stay down to it. The use of a more lofted club also helps.

An upright swing should be used for a downhill lie, too. Hold the hands a shade higher than usual, a position that promotes an upright swing, open the stance a bit and don't be afraid of cutting across the ball a little. Stand closer, grip shorter, and make the swing shorter. All this tends toward control and also toward keeping the face from closing and smothering the shot.

Since you expect, and probably will get, a drift to the right, aim the shot to the left. This, of course, is just the reverse of playing from an uphill lie.

ABOVE THE BALL

Hitting a ball while standing above it presents another set of problems. This is, perhaps, the most awkward of all positions and the hardest of the four shots from uneven lies. But it's not at all impossible.

Since the tendency here is to fall into the shot and to slice, take the common-sense precautions against each. Bend the knees more than usual so that you "sit down" to the ball. Keep the weight chiefly on the heels so as to keep it well back. Take a longer grip on the club so as to be certain the club head will reach the ball. Close the face slightly to counteract the tendency to slice. Aim a little to the left to take care of a probable fade on the shot. And, at all costs, *stay down to the ball throughout the swing.* The slightest rise invites immediate disaster.

BELOW THE BALL

Standing below the ball as you hit it is a much easier proposition. It is very similar to playing from an uphill lie and the treatment is largely the same.

The big difference is that when standing below the ball

you tend to fall back and away from it. Therefore, when addressing it, be sure that your weight is on the balls of your feet rather than your heels. This is about the only thing you can do to offset the pull of gravity.

Otherwise the swing is about the same as for an uphill lie. Shorten the grip, the pivot, and the swing, use a firm left hand, and aim a little to the right to counteract a tendency to pull or hook.

Uneven lies are disquieting and annoying to the average golfer when he has to make anything like a full shot from them. Usually he doesn't have much of an idea of how to play them. But to have a general idea of what is required is half the battle. Every golfer should learn how to play them, for they are a part of the game.

HEAVY AND CLOSE LIES

A close lie is the dub's graveyard shot. This is so because he simply doesn't know what to do with it. Time and again we have seen golfers dig into the ground on their tee shots, when the player gives himself the best possible lie, and then try to scoop the ball out of a tight lie or a divot hole.

These are directly opposite to the things they should be doing. A ball can and should be swept off a tee. But the closer it lies on the ground, the more the player should *hit down* through it. Thousands of players have seen Joe Kirkwood's trick shots. Few, however, profit from the shot in which he steps on the ball and then hits it 200 yards. All Kirkwood does is try to hit the ball deeper into the hole.

On all close lies hit down on the ball, using a more upright swing.

A heavy clover lie on the fairway is another minor problem. Contact with the club face is not clean and the ball tends to dip low if hit with a normal swing. It is best, from a clover lie, to underclub and try to take the ball a bit clean. Never hit down on it.

Playing a ball out from under low-hanging tree branches is a tantalizing shot that we all have had to make at some time or other and, we fear, will have to make again.

Obviously, the important thing here is to get the ball out without hitting the branches. In order to get the low ball we want, we should sacrifice everything else for it. Use a club with a straighter face than the shot seems to call for, put virtually all the weight on the left foot, and don't pivot. These three things will insure a low ball, insofar as it can be insured. And they are all you can do. If your shot is to a green that can be approached by a run-up, so much the better. If not, well, it's just too bad.

PART FOUR

CHAPTER SIXTEEN

GENERAL OBSERVATIONS AND CONCLUSIONS

THIS BOOK has been directed primarily toward the purpose given in the introduction, which is to "straighten you out," or help you help yourself. We have listed all the bad shots, explained what caused them, and given the cure for them. We would like now to set down some general thoughts on the golf swing.

Chief among these is that there are literally millions of men and women playing golf today who never give themselves a chance to play it well. There is no good reason why a person who plays golf with any degree of regularity should be unable to break 100, or 90 if he plays quite frequently.

The main reason for consistently high golf scores, we believe, is that all but a very small percentage of those who play the game put themselves in such a position at the top of the backswing that they can't deliver a good shot. In other words, they don't give themselves a chance at the top of the swing to play good golf.

We will venture to say that we could put Sam Snead, Byron Nelson, or any other top-ranking professional into a position at the top from which he couldn't break 80. Such a position could be any one of a hundred we see in Sunday morning foursomes at golf clubs all over the country. Is it any wonder, then, that the struggling duffers in these four-somes continue for years to be no more than struggling duffers? They never give themselves a chance.

The same could well be said of two other parts of the swing: The grip and the first movement of the downswing. For these two, plus the position at the top, constitute the three prime fundamentals of golf. If these are performed correctly a good shot must follow. If any one of the three is incorrect, the chance of a good shot is diminished. If all three are wrong—as they are with thousands of players—then a bad shot is inevitable.

Golf, we believe, can be made as simple as that.

THREE MOVEMENTS

The proper grip goes far toward insuring one vitally important thing. This is that the face of the club will be at right angles to the direction line at the moment of impact, that the face will be neither open nor closed. Either an open or closed face at impact will bring trouble of one kind or another, whereas the good, straight shot can be delivered only with a face that is square to the line. With an improper grip it is very difficult to bring the club face square to the line at the ball. Yet hundreds of thousands of players use wrong grips all the time, have used them for years, and can't understand why they never improve. We repeat: They don't give themselves a chance.

A correct position at the top of the backswing probably is the biggest factor in producing a good shot. If you reach the top properly you are then coiled and set to deliver a blow of great power and one in the right direction, which is from the inside out. It still is possible to spoil the swing even after reaching the top correctly. But spoiling it from that position is much less likely.

On the other hand, if we reach the top in a wrong position, then the delivery of a powerful, inside-out blow becomes difficult. It can be done but only by one or more lightning-fast compensations on the way down, and by an expert, at that.

Since it is just as easy physically for you to reach the top correctly as it is to reach it incorrectly, why not do it the right way? In short, why not give yourself a chance?

The only barriers are in not knowing what the right position is and in wrong habits formed by swinging wrong for a long time. These habits must be broken down and new habits substituted. But this can be done. Don't think it can't.

The third prime fundamental, which is the first movement of the downswing, is the clincher. If the grip and the position at the top both are correct, the swing can be spoiled by a bad start down. But a good shot also can be clinched by the right start down. And the right start is by all odds the easiest of the trio of fundamentals.

Once this movement is made accurately, a bad shot is all but impossible. This movement eliminates the last possibility of throwing the club head outside the line and also the last chance of uncocking the wrists too soon and expending the power before the ball is reached.

With the proper grip and position at the top and then

with this correct first movement in the downswing, we will defy anyone to hit either too soon or from the outside in. Those are the things that ruin most shots.

FROM THE TOP

Hitting too soon (hitting from the top) is without doubt one of the most common errors the game knows, and it completely spoils any possibility of a good shot. It throws the club outside the line and uses up power at the beginning of the downswing that should be saved until the finish.

This hitting from the top is caused, as we have mentioned, by the wrong position at the top and/or by a wrong first movement in the downswing. As we have explained, these both can be eliminated and when they are, there is not only no temptation to hit from the top but no possibility of it.

It is peculiar, in a way, that hitting too soon is a fault more pronounced in golf than in any other sport. A good analogy is the throwing of a baseball. No one, in throwing a ball, releases it while his arm is still drawn back. Such a thing never occurs to him. The ball leaves his hand only after the body and the arm have been brought forward. A fisherman doesn't cast a fly while the rod is behind him. The fly is released after the rod has been whipped forward. If a bowler let go of the ball at the top of his backswing he would soon be barred for smashing up the alley and crippling other bowlers. Yet the golfer's strong tendency is to hit right from the top. The big reason for this is that he is not in the right position at the top. If he were, he would not let fly nearly so soon.

THAT LEFT HAND

A great deal has been written in our chapters on corrections about the position of the right wrist being under the shaft at the top. Perhaps we have written so much about it that the reader may develop a contempt for the left hand and left wrist. Such was by no means the intention.

The position of the right wrist was stressed only to be certain that the player gets it out of the way so the left hand and left wrist can dominate. This is necessary because in a right-handed person the right hand is so much stronger than the left. Unless sharp measures are taken against the stronger right, it will overwhelm the weaker left.

The left, however, is the important hand and wrist. Perhaps we should say the left would be the important hand if we gave it a chance. The left is the one that does most of the swinging. It is the one that brings the club to the proper position from which the right hand can deliver the punch and the power. It is the left arm that must be kept straight to insure a constant radius for the arc of the swing. And it is the left arm that must not collapse at impact. It won't collapse if we give it room to swing through unobstructed and don't dominate it with the right hand.

At the top it is the left hand that must have the stronger grip on the club and that must remain in control until the hands are almost hip high on the downswing. It is the left wrist at the top that governs the position of the right elbow we have heard and read so much about over the years. You've all been told, I am sure, that the right elbow should be kept close to the side and pointed toward the ground. We've been told it should be close enough so that a rolled-up handkerchief can be kept in the right armpit throughout the swing. That's not quite true. Keeping the right elbow so close tends to cramp the swing and make it too flat. However, if the left wrist is under the shaft at the top, the elbow will then fly out like a wing, which is wrong. If the right wrist is under the shaft, the elbow very naturally will be kept fairly close and pointing to the ground.

It is not enough for an instructer to say, however, "Keep your right elbow close to your side," without telling you *how* to keep it there. That is like a football coach telling an end to block a halfback, without having first instructed him how to do it.

Another thing made difficult by having the left wrist under the shaft at the top is keeping the left arm straight. If you will take a club and swing it to the top a few times, first with the left wrist under and then with the right wrist under, you will see the difference. The bending back of the left hand to get the left wrist under definitely affects the arm muscles and tends to make the elbow bend. This immediately sets up a train of difficulties that will have to be corrected or compensated for if the ball is to be hit right.

A firm left hand and wrist also are necessary so that the stronger right hand will not overpower them, throw the club head outside the line on the way down, and close the face of the club. So long as the left is firm and remains firm right through the ball, the chances of hooking, pulling, smothering, or slicing will be greatly reduced. But once the left loses its contest with the right, look for trouble—quickly.

BREAKING BAD HABITS

One of the great difficulties in correcting the many movements in the golf swing is the tremendous power exerted by habit. Players who have been doing things wrong for years or even months will revert to their usual action after a correction has been made. Then they show no improvement and wonder why. The funny part of this is that the player will not believe he has reverted. He has to be shown. It has to be proved to him.

Take, for instance, the chap who has been using a hook grip for a long time. His left hand is well over on top of the shaft and his right hand is low. Thumb and forefinger V's on both hands point well to the right of the right shoulder. Chances are that this player is having all kinds of trouble— hooking, smothering, or pulling.

He goes to a pro, who starts by moving his hands to the correct position to the left. Improvement follows. Within a week though, our friend is back in the same old faults, hitting the ball just as badly as he ever did, and cursing just as much. He goes again to the pro who sees at once that the hands are back in their old position, and he tells the player.

But does the player believe him? He does not. He will stand there and argue with the pro that his hands are not in their old position, that they are exactly where the pro placed them so carefully only a week ago, and that something else must be causing the trouble. Only after a great deal of patience and explanation can the pro convince his pupil that his hands are still wrong.

This incident is an old story to the pros. They've been through it thousands of times. You may even have had the experience yourself.

The point is that unless you are eternally vigilant in mak-ing corrections you will also unmake them and revert to your old bad habits.

This can happen with any number of actions. For in-stance, you may have formed the habit of opening your left hand at the top of the swing. You are told to keep it closed and you start to do exactly that. But before you know it the hand is opening again—and you don't realize it. When someone finally tells you about it, your first inclination is to deny it. You have been intending to keep the hand closed and have been thinking right along that it is closed. But it hasn't been.

You may not think that you sway, or dip, or have the left wrist under the shaft. Yet you may be doing all these things. You may believe you are starting the backswing all in one piece, that you have your hands head high at the top, and that the shaft is pointing across the line of flight. Yet you may not be doing any of them.

All of which means that in making any changes you must keep checking them to be certain there is no reversion. This checking must be done accurately. Don't just *think* you are doing the right things. Use the checks we have given: with a lamp and shadows on the wall, the grass test, the shadow test with the sun, the peg test for an outside-in swing, etc. Use the observation of a companion too. A second party can tell you such things as whether the club face is open or closed at the top and whether you are swaying, better than you can yourself.

In any event, keep checking. No change you make will stay with you automatically. You must keep at it until the new position itself becomes a habit. Then you are reasonably safe for a time.

TWO CLASSES OF BAD SHOTS

In setting out to correct any bad shots you may have, or to check your swing generally, it will help to have an over-all picture of the faulty side of the game.

This faulty side, of course, is made up entirely of the nine bad shots. It is well to remember, however, that the causes of these nine shots fall into two well-defined categories. One is the position of the club face at the moment of impact with the ball: that is, whether the face is open, closed, or square to the line the club head is following. The other is the *point on the ball* at which the club head makes contact; whether it strikes the upper part of the ball, the back of the ball, or the lower part.

For example, slicing, hooking, pushing, pulling, and smothering depend on the position of the club face. Topping, skying, and sclaffing depend on where the club head strikes the ball. The ninth bad shot—shanking—also would come under the second category, even though the club head doesn't meet the ball at all.

Slicing and pushing are the result of an open face; hooking and pulling are the consequence of a closed face; and smothering is the inevitable penalty of a face closed so much that it is hooded. If you are troubled by any of these five shots (and not by the others) you know that your club face is misbehaving. That is the root of your distress. Your first move, therefore, is to find out what is causing the club face to misbehave.

You know, if you have read this far, that the position of the club face at impact is governed by only two things: The grip and the position at the top of the backswing. Take a faulty grip with the hands too far to one side or the other, and trouble is sure to follow. Or take the correct grip and use the wrong wrist action in getting to the top, and the trouble can be just as great.

This club face position is, of course, tied in closely with the direction from which the club head approaches the ball—whether it comes from the inside out or from the outside in. This is true of all five bad shots that are caused by club-face position, except smothering. If your club face is actually hooded, then it will make no difference whether the swing is inside out or outside in.

A slice, for instance, is caused by a face that is open to the direction the club head is following. A hook comes when the face is closed to the direction the club head is moving. A push occurs when the face is open to the *intended* direction line but square to the line the club head is following. A pull eventuates when the exact reverse is true—the face being closed to the *intended* direction line but square to the path of the club head.

To go back to the slice, you will get one if your club face is open to the direction the club head is following, regardless of whether that direction is correct or not. If it is correct, that is, from the inside out, and following along the intended direction line as it meets the ball, you will still slice if the face is open. That's what happens when top-flight players slice intentionally. Their swing is perfect, but they take pains to insure a slightly open face.

That's not what happens to all the rest of us though. Our swing isn't perfect (not quite), we come at the ball from the outside in, and we have an open face too. That way lies madness.

The general solution to all of this, naturally, is first to insure good control of the club face position by taking the proper grip and then by being certain that the right wrist is under the shaft at the top causing a half-closed face at the top. This will bring a face square to the line at impact. If, after that, we take the steps to correct our swing so that it will be always from the inside out, a large percentage of our difficulties will have been solved.

As to the other category of bad-shot causes, the point on the ball where the club head makes contact, that is entirely different. We have seen in our earlier chapters that topping, skying, and sclaffing are nearly always accompanied by a sharply descending downswing. Or, in the pro's vernacular, chopping.

Whenever we bring the club head down to the ball at a sharp angle instead of sweeping it along nearly parallel to the ground, we are heading for the danger zone. In the correct swing the club head moves close to the ground for some little distance and hits the ball in the back. With a swing like that there is little danger of hitting behind the ball or under it and not much chance of hitting it on top. But with a chopping stroke you can do any of those things and are very likely to do one of them.

If the chop brings the club head down on top of the ball, it means a certain top. You will literally drive the ball into the ground. If you chop and manage to hit the ball square in the back anyway, you'll get a very low ball. If your chop comes down a shade lower, hitting under the ball, you'll get a skied shot. If you hit still farther back, you'll hit the ground before the ball, which is a sclaff.

So, if you are a fairly consistent topper, skier, or sclaffer, examine yourself first for a chopping downswing. You're pretty sure to find it. Then set about getting rid of it.

We have learned that a chop usually is the result of a quick lift of the club on the backswing. The easiest and surest way to eliminate a quick lift is to start the backswing *all in one piece.* If you do that you simply can't lift. Then, since you won't chop without a quick lift, the dangers of topping, skying, and sclaffing will virtually disappear.

We hope, through listing the bad shots, explaining their causes, giving their cures, and setting the right path for you to follow, we have helped you. We also hope, by the analysis we have given, we have convinced you that playing good golf is not a hopeless task. The game is not as complicated as we all have been led to believe. We weren't led deliberately or maliciously to such a belief. We were led there by a great lack of knowledge. The golf swing simply was executed faster than the eye could follow or the brain record its movements. Therefore, the best golfers did things they didn't know they did and taught things they didn't do. No one possibly can blame them for that. The fact that we know now so much more about the golf swing than we knew 15 or 20 years ago is due strictly to the advance of science. The ultra-fast motion-picture camera, that produces slow-motion pictures, has cleared away the fog and provided proof that had been lacking. More use of it, we believe—much more—should be made.

INDEX

Above the ball, standing, 167-168

Backswing, club position at top of, 21-23, 174-175
  flat, 66
  head position in, 21
  left-shoulder position in, 32
  position at top of, 17-20, 33, 50, 88-89
  right-hand pickup, 66-67
  right-knee position in, 82
  starting, 26-28, 92, 117
  weight shift in, 28
  wrist "break" in, 28-29
  wrist position in, 23-24, 48-49
Bad habits, correcting, 179-181
Bad shots, correcting, 181-182
Below the ball, standing, 167-168
Bent-grass greens, 155-156
Birdies, increase in, 141-142
Burke, Jack, 7

Chipping, position for, 138
  variety of irons for, 139
  wrist action in, 134-138
Chopping, 108, 183-184
  test for, 82
Close lies, 168-169
Club face, closed, 60-62
  bad backswing cause of, 66-68
  bad grip cause of, 63-65
  causes of, 63
  correct position of, 23-25
  hooded, 86
Club head, turnover of, 108-111
Cut-shot artist, 125-126

Diegel, Leo, 7
Downhill lie, 166-167
Downswing, 33-34, 175-176
  hip-turn in, 35-37, 115-117
  mistakes in, 32, 108-110, 113-115

Explosion shot, 160-162

Finger calluses, reason for, 4

Golf, three fundamentals of, 174
Grip, correct, 4-6, 46, 68
  advantage of, 7
  firm, importance of, 8-9
  importance of, 3, 174, 182
  testing, 4
  wrong, 7-8, 46-47, 86-87

Hagen, Walter, 153
Head lifting, 72-74
  test for, 74-76
Heavy lies, 169
Hitting from the top, 54-55
  cause of, 176
Hooking, cause of, 60, 182
  corrections for, 70
  right-hand domination in, 68-70
  (See also Club face, closed)
Hutchison, Jock, 7

Iron shots, 129-131

Jones, Bob, 7, 153

Kirkwood, Joe, 168

Left hand, importance of, 177-179
Lofted clubs, 159

McSpaden, Jug, 143

Nelson, Byron, 30

Open face, causes of, 46-48
Overlapping grip, 4-7

Pillow test, 30-31
Pronation, 110-111
Pulling, 60, 62
  causes of, 91-92
  club facing wrong, 94-95, 182
  poor pivot, 94
  sway, 93-94
  weight shift, 93
  wrong downswing, 95-97
  wrong wrist position, 94

INDEX

Pushing, 45
  causes of, 98-99, 182
    ball, position of, 103
    flat swing, 102-103
    sway to left, 100-101
    corrections for, 104
Putter, loft of, 155
  weight of, 154-155
Putting, backswing in, 152
  body position in, 152
  club-face position in, 143-144
  experimentation in, 142
  grip for, 145-147
  weight distribution in, 153
  wrist "break" in, 148
Putting aim, 154
Putting stroke, 147-152

Rough shots, clubs used in, 159-160
  judgment in, 157-159
  technique in, 159

Sand traps (see Traps)
Sand wedge, 160
Sclaffing, cause of, 113-115, 117-118
  correction for, 115, 118-119
Shanking, 121
  causes of, 122, 124-125
  correcting, 125, 126
  cut shots in, 125-126
  fear of, 120-121
Short pitches, 131
  essentials of, 132
  foot position for, 138
  topping, 134
  wrist action in, 131-132
Shoulder raising, tension cause of, 72-74
Skying, causes of, 105-106
  corrections for, 106, 108, 112
  grass test for, 106
Slice, killer, 45-46
  tail-end, 45
Slicing, causes of, 44, 182-183
  corrections for, 58-59
  (See also Grip; Swing, outside-in)
Smothering, cause of, 84-86, 89-90, 182
    bad position at top, 88-89
    poor grip, 86-87

corrections for, 90
degrees of, 86
Snead, Sam, 30
Stance, body position in, 10-13
  closed, 13-14
  open, 13-14
  relaxed position essential to, 14-15
  square, 13-14
  weight distribution, 14-15
Swaying, 31-32
  forward, 105-106
  left, 100-101
    causes of, 101-102
    guarding against, 102
  right, 76-77
  test for, 78-79
Swing, 76
  "inside-out", 16-17, 25
  outside-in, causes of, 50, 95-97
    club position in, 54
    elbow position in, 53
    left-arm position in, 53
    left-hand position in, 53-54
    loss of control in, 54
    open-face club in, 54
    pivot in, 51
    shoulder position in, 51-53
    swaying in, 53
    testing, 55-56
    weight transference in, 51
  raised arc, 79-81
  (See also Backswing)

Tension, 72-74
Topping, causes of, 71
  corrections for, 83
  (See also Head lifting; Swaying; Swing, raised arc of)
Traps, explosion shot out of, 160-162
  judgment in shooting out of, 163-164
  swing in shooting out of, 162

Uphill lies, 165-166
  underclubbing on, 166

Vardon, Harry, 7, 53

Weight transference, 20-21